4

GAUTAM SACHDEVA

# THE END OF
# SEPARATION

Finding peace and equanimity through our relationships

D1716058

YogiImpressions®

**YogiImpressions**®

THE END OF SEPARATION

First published in India in 2015 by

**Yogi Impressions Books Pvt. Ltd.**

1711, Centre 1, World Trade Centre,

Cuffe Parade, Mumbai 400 005, India.

Website: www.yogiimpressions.com

First Edition, July 2015

Copyright © 2015 by Gautam Sachdeva

Book Design: www.designpinkindia.com

ISBN 978-93-82742-29-6

Printed at: Parksons Graphics, Mumbai

# Homage to the Lineage of Masters

| Siddharameshwar Maharaj (1888-1936) | Nisargadatta Maharaj (1897-1981) | Ramesh Balsekar (1917-2009) |

*'Gurur Brahma, Gurur Vishnu,*
*Gurur Devo Maheshwara.*
*Gurur Sakshat Parabrahma,*
*Tasmai Shri Gurave Namah.'*

The Guru is Brahma, the Guru is Vishnu,
The Guru is the Lord Shiva.
The Guru is the Supreme Reality,
I bow in reverence to that Guru.

The Guru is Consciousness.
Consciousness is all there is.

*Dedicated to my mother*
*Santosh Sachdeva*

# CONTENTS

# INTRODUCTION

What a human being desires most is happiness. With the passage of time, he realises that happiness which depends on the pleasures of life is a fleeting happiness, as pleasures themselves are momentary. What he actually desires is a true, more permanent happiness – one that is not dependent on pleasures.

What is this true happiness that one is seeking? To put it simply, it is nothing but peace of mind.

If true happiness cannot be found in the flow of life that alternates between pleasure and pain, then where is it to be found?

It is to be found in one's *attitude* to life. And one's attitude to life means one's attitude towards the 'other'. For daily living means 'my' relationship with the 'other', whoever the 'other' may be – parent, child, colleague, friend, or even a stranger. So what gives me peace of mind? I have peace of mind when my relationship with the 'other' is harmonious. And when is my relationship with others harmonious? It is when I am comfortable with myself and with others. And when am I comfortable with myself and others? It is when I know that we are, as my spiritual teacher Ramesh Balsekar would say, all 'instruments' through whom the same energy functions; just as it is the same electricity that functions through various gadgets in the kitchen, enabling each gadget to perform what it is programmed to do.

When there is a deep understanding that nobody truly 'does' anything but it is the same Divine energy i.e. Consciousness, which functions through each one of us and brings about what it does through each human being – a sense of relaxation starts setting in. For the view is no longer a split one where each one thinks he is solely responsible for his output.

This sense of relaxation annihilates the venomous sting of hatred towards others, for they are now seen in light of who they truly are. Hatred, condemnation and blame start diminishing as it is seen that everyone (including oneself) is a product of their genes and conditioning. More importantly, pride, arrogance, guilt and shame also start diminishing. No feeling of pride and arrogance for my good actions, or guilt and shame for my so-called bad actions. No hatred towards others for their actions. Absence of pride, arrogance, guilt, shame and so on, means peace of mind.

> The self, deluded by egoism,
> thinketh: 'I am the doer'.
>
> – *The Bhagavad Gita* (III-27, 28)

The juicer does not 'do' anything, nor does the toaster. The electricity is the only doer as such. The same Consciousness functions through each of us. With this understanding, the true meaning of 'universal brotherhood' is realised; not one where only those belonging to our religion are considered our brothers.

*Rnanubandhana* is a core concept of Indian karmic thought that literally translates as 'bondage of debt' (of relationships). It refers to the 'cosmic debt based on a former relationship'. According to this concept, a relationship can 'happen' between two individuals through the mechanism of Rnanubandhana. Karma (action and reaction) is due to this debt and can occur only if there exists a past bondage of debt between them. Whether or not we believe in past births and Rnanubandhana, the fact is that daily living means one's relationship with others, unless one is an ascetic sitting in a cave in the mountains.

On Rnanubandhana, the revered and much venerated Indian mystic Sai Baba of Shirdi has said:

*'Unless there is some relationship or connection, nobody goes anywhere. If any men or creatures come to you, do not discourteously drive them away but receive them well... if anybody wants money from you and you are not inclined to give, do not give but do not bark like a dog. Let anybody speak hundreds of things against you, do not resent by giving any bitter reply. If you tolerate such things you will certainly be happy. Let the world go topsy-turvy, you remain where you are. Standing in your own place, look on calmly at the show of all things passing before you. Demolish the wall of difference that separates you from Me, and then the road for our meeting will be clear and open... God is the sole Proprietor... His Will be done and He will show us the way... It is on account of rnanubandhana that we have come together, let us love and serve each other and be happy.'\**

---

\* *Shri Sai Satcharitra* – G. R. Dabholkar, Shri Sai Baba Sansthan, Shirdi. English translation by N. V. Gunaji.

While I had no idea there was such a word defining this concept, it dawned on me that what Ramesh Balsekar spoke about was exactly what Sai Baba was saying – except that he did not use the word 'Rnanubandhana'. What's more, his teaching did not take into consideration the existence of a 'former relationship' preceding this birth. After all, the ego in a particular birth dies with the death of the body. The ego is not reborn. Therefore, if nobody does anything and all there is, is the will of God, then there was no question of a 'personal' action/reaction loop of karma.

As the sage Vimalananda* said: 'Self-identification with one's actions converts them into karma by binding the ego down more tightly to the limited, temporary personality.'

So practical was the teaching and its approach to relationships as presented by Ramesh, that it ultimately delivered peace of mind in daily living.

This book is comprised of essays, plus some questions and answers, that touch upon different aspects of relationships – relationships with others, our relationship with ourselves, and our relationship with 'what is' – all pointing back to who we *truly* are, and not what we *appear* to be.

When this inherent interconnectedness is seen in the light of total clarity, we are free of all the shackles that bind us down to relationships where we consider ourselves as separate from others, and heap judgement after judgement upon them. The *bandhas* (bonds) are then snapped as swiftly as Alexander the Great cut through the 'impossible to untie' Gordian Knot with a single stroke of his sword.

---

* *Aghora: At the Left Hand of God* – Robert E. Svoboda. There is a detailed chapter on Rnanubandhana, as explained by Vimalananda.

Karma is now pure action, without the taint of ownership and self-identification with the action. 'Not my will, but Thine, be done,' as Jesus said. What shines forth is true Love – unfettered and unconditional. There is no 'other' to hate. When there is no 'other' to hate, it truly means that there is no 'other'. And when there is no 'other', there is no 'me' as separate from the 'other'.

There is no 'other' to love as well, as a separate individual, for all boundaries have been annihilated. Everything is now one cohesive, harmonious Whole.

Consciousness is all there truly is.

# JOURNEYS AT THE OFFICE DESK

My spiritual teacher, Ramesh Balsekar, would often say that peace of mind cannot be found in the flow of life but rather in our attitude to life and towards the 'other'. Because in daily living, our relationship with others plays an important role.

An office or similar work environment is an ideal ground from which to witness the interplay of various kinds of relationships. In retrospect, I can clearly see that I learnt a lot about people and inter-human relationships through my years at work. Little wonder then that Ramesh, himself a banker for 37 years, was always curious to know how things were at work, whenever we would meet.

We all have our stories to tell, and here's mine as far as my work life is concerned. The intention is to share how I now view all that happened at and through work, in light of the teaching of non-duality. I can clearly see that the conditioning I received during my working years provided a fertile ground on which the seeds of non-duality were planted. Besides the share of life's experiences that we all face, work for me provided the additional facet of being exposed to a multitude of relationships. In my professional life I had already experienced what I heard Ramesh speak of, when I visited him years later. It was hardly a surprise that I took to the teaching like a fish takes to water.

It is famously said that 'there are more authors than readers' and adding to the heap was easy. As I ran a spiritual publishing house, it was not difficult to find a publisher!

**The early years**

I started going to the office during my third year in higher college, when I was 20. Although my father had passed away when I was 14, the advertising agency that he founded was still functioning. It was being run by the team who were present at the time of his passing. My mother, who had until then been a typical Indian housewife, had also been visiting the office during those six years. Although not knowledgeable about advertising, she played the role of being present to handle whatever challenges the company would face to the best of her ability, while the team was busy handling the clients and work at hand. Bringing up three teenaged children as well as going to work must have been a challenging task, to say the least.

When I turned 24, it seemed that all hell had broken loose on the work front. One fine evening, the management informed my mother that they were leaving to start their own advertising venture. They said they would hire someone in their place to run the show. It was all so sudden and unexpected – a bolt from the blue! However, I was given a hint of this a few days earlier when I went to make a presentation to a client. He was someone close to the management. When he mentioned their plans to me

(I still can't fathom why!), I thought it was such an outlandish idea that I actually went and blurted it out to them. I got no response so it seemed clear to me that it was just the client's fantasy running wild. But from that point on, the only thing I was clear on was that one should be aware that anything is possible. And quite often, that 'anything' was the polaric opposite of the current situation at hand – something one could hardly imagine. Life has a habit of giving you exactly that which you *think* you don't need. Or perhaps, that which would never cross your mind in your wildest dreams.

My mother and I were all shook up, as we knew it would most likely spell the end of the business and therefore the family's income. Nobody knew the clients besides the management – there were no other relationships in place.

Worse things were in store over the coming days. Close on the heels of this development came another big surprise – they sent out invites to all our clients stating that they were starting their own advertising agency and invited them for the opening of their new office. And, we only found this out when one of our clients forwarded me an invite asking what was going on! It did seem quite cheeky of them at first, but then it was perhaps the most logical thing for them to do, in hindsight. After all, they were the ones who had built up the relationships with the clients over the years. However, at that time, it felt unethical as they had been with the agency for so many years, through thick and thin. If they had at least informed us that they would be sending out the invites, we would have been better prepared, as until then we had not informed the clients that they were leaving.

We feared that all the clients would shift their accounts as there was no one else left in the agency whom they had confidence in. Don't ask me why and how it happened, but we were fortunate that only one of the big clients chose to shift their account.

It was then that my recently married brother-in-law, who had an advertising background, was roped in to helm the ship. However, this too provided relief only in the short term as it was to last only for a few months. After the initial few months, he was clear that as he was in charge of affairs he deserved a stake in the company, else he would quit. Asking for a stake was fair, but he wanted the majority share. We almost agreed as no other option was available to us. However, our auditor strongly advised us against this option no matter what the cost, as it would mean losing control over the family business. He said something which gave me much strength in those days: 'Nobody is indispensable. People come and go. Organisations tend to carry on, no matter who leaves. After all, it did continue even after your father.' However, this was more of an intellectual strength. When your income is tied tightly to others, then you certainly think they are indispensable – more so when you are 24 and have not really been exposed to running a business – even if it's a small family business.

We were in a dilemma: *How would we run the show if he left? Whom would the clients have faith in now? After the turbulence in the agency a few months ago, what could we tell them now? What were we to do?* In this situation, my mother turned to her guru for advice. He told her to leave the problem at his doorstep, and let the Source take care of the rest.

We shored up the courage and decided not to budge, thanks largely to his encouragement as well as the auditor's advice. This new position taken by us must have surprised my then brother-in-law. For, we had even agreed to a 50:50 stake in our naivete, without consulting the auditors. Fortunately (as usual in hindsight, of course), he insisted on getting not just half of the stake but a majority, and so stopped coming to work.

Here we were. The luxury of choices was no longer available. Either we would have to shut shop, or I would have to try my hand at running the business for whatever it was worth.

Suddenly, I found myself heading a staff of about 30 people, all of them older than me. When I look back I can see that it turned out to be a fertile ground to 'practice the teaching' as far as human relationships were concerned, as Ramesh would later say. Up until then I had not been exposed to Ramesh's teaching. That's why I realised, when I started visiting Ramesh and attending his talks, that his teaching was a validation of my life's experiences thus far.

I remember an incident when a new client had come over for a meeting and walked into my cabin. He kept waiting without speaking much. After talking shop, I asked him if I could help him with his requirements, and what services was he looking for from our agency. He said it was quite alright, and continued to sit silently in his chair. This was a bit odd, I thought. Both of us were quiet as we had run out of conversation, and I was at my wit's end as to how to take this forward. After 10 minutes passed, he asked me, 'Why is your boss taking so long to come?' He was quite flabbergasted when I told him that I was indeed the boss.

The situation I found myself in at work was a daunting one. I was intimidated and fearful about retaining the business. On top of that, the entire working world around me including my colleagues, suppliers, and clients, were older than me. Some by four decades! To add to that, I was more of an introvert. My shyness was often misconstrued as snobbishness. Being chubby in my school days had not helped my self-esteem either. I was not comfortable with the slightest amount of attention. I even remember dashing from my building elevator to the car, lest I be seen in my boy scouts uniform that we had to wear once a week. And so, I found myself between a rock and a hard place. I was hardly the young lad brimming with confidence eager to meet the challenges of business as a CEO. Just what I thought I did not need was forced my way. Yet, things gradually tilted in my favour, by the grace of God.

At first, the hardest part for me was to deal with the clients. That was where our bread and butter came from, and if they were not happy and decided to leave, that would mean the end of the show. The survival issue had raised its ugly head once again in my life, as it did when my father had passed away. There was no question of running away from this lion; there never is. As the Buddhists say, all fears are nothing but the fear of death. This was a very real fear. And the clients were rolling the dice! Unhappy clients meant departing clients, which meant departing money, and no money ultimately meant no food, shelter and clothing, which basically meant the game was over. This was the thought-process my 24-year old brain was configured with.

At my first meeting, I remember walking into a client's office. It was an impressive conference room, but my jaw dropped when I saw a table that could perhaps seat 16 people, with him sitting at the end of it. God does have a sense of humour I thought – no table of a lesser size would do for my first meeting. I was quite nervous and wondered whether I would end up making a fool of myself. Finally, the meeting got over and I silently breathed a sigh of relief. When I was at the door, the client turned around and said to me: 'Gautam, as long as I get what I need from you and your team, I am happy.' And that relationship endured right through my advertising career. In fact, it became our biggest account for quite a number of years.

As time rolled by, I began to realise that I was generally likeable. In fact, I got along with practically everyone, and it wasn't that I was expending any effort to do so. I got invited to clients' homes to have dinner with their families, and I got invited to suppliers' homes to have lunch with theirs. I think the main reason was that I did not really get in anyone's way. I was, by and large, an amiable chap. Everyone in the office was allowed to express their views. I also had an open-door policy, in the sense that my cabin-door was never closed and they could walk in anytime. I even recall having pasted a quotation on my cabin door that said: 'Are you part of the problem or have you come here with a solution?' The staff made me remove it as they felt it put them under tremendous pressure before entering my cabin. But, at least the mystery of their stopping short of the cabin and returning to their desks was solved.

My colleagues did not perceive me as a threat, and that really helped as otherwise they might have had a hard time taking this kid being their boss seriously! I rarely raised my voice or screamed and shouted. This reminds me of a recent situation at work.

Two colleagues were at loggerheads; one much senior than the other. There was a lot of screaming and shouting, and tempers flared. The senior was handling the situation roughly, and it was uncalled for. It was the junior's last day, and he hadn't done a proper handover. This had riled the senior, and he got aggressive. The situation got out of hand and the junior stormed out of the office without looking back, and that was the end of things. I felt bad as it was not good to leave the organisation in this manner. The same evening, I called the senior in, heard him out, and expressed to him that while he was acting in the best interests of the company, being the senior, he could have handled the situation with more tact. Perhaps the junior who left might yet be needed in case the new recruit got stuck in some work aspects. It's always good to have a healthy parting. Now, that option was a dead-end. Besides, that aggression had rattled the women in the office. What struck me was the senior's response. His eyes momentarily went moist. He said that in his earlier job, work would get done only when his senior would kick the cabin door open, and scream and shout expletives. He said he had absorbed that conditioning and thought that was the only way to deal with subordinates. And, he also wondered aloud why I never did the same. I said I couldn't, because it simply wasn't my nature or my conditioning.

Over the months, work drew me out and I started getting comfortable with people from diverse backgrounds, age groups, income groups, and nationalities. I recently came across a word that perhaps best describes the change. The conditioning at work morphed me into an 'ambivert' – a cross between an introvert and extrovert. But at heart I was an introvert. In fact, I even won a white card in school for being 'the most well-behaved boy in class'. That was strange, I thought. All I did was keep quiet, and that too I did not expend any effort in order to keep quiet; yet I got rewarded. The Lord works in mysterious ways!

The days in advertising turned out to be quite exciting. I used to be in the office till about midnight twice a week. The reason for this was that our Creative Director was from one of India's leading ad agencies, and he would moonlight for us after finishing his work. He spearheaded the creative team, and we all learnt a lot from him in those formative years. While I found it easier over time to handle clients, my interest was more in the creative side of the business. So, I really didn't mind the long hours at work when the creative brainstorming would take place in the late evenings.

Our Creative Director used to insist that the client servicing team fight tooth and nail to hold up the creatives that the agency was presenting, and it held us in good stead. We were assigned a lot of below-the-line work for some of India's leading brands, and business started pouring in. At the same time, our egos were reined in by the Source, for we were not really able to break through to become the agency for their mainline advertising. We earned the reputation of being a small but quality-conscious firm.

I remember an incident regarding the creatives that was quite impactful. We had pitched for an account and the client had loved our work. The artworks were ready to go to print. The contract was signed. Everyone was thrilled. And then, at the final hour, the client called up and said his wife was of the opinion that the colour scheme of the campaign be changed from a black/yellow combination to a black/red one. Suddenly, there was trouble in paradise. My Creative Director felt that, for very valid reasons, it would destroy the sanctity of the entire creative strategy, and said we had no option but to insist we adhere to the original scheme. And, as he rightly said, 'We don't teach them how to create their product, so why should they (especially their wives) teach us how to create ours?' Then, of course, he expected me to go and tell the client that!

Anyway, such one-sided battles are lost long before they are even fought. All gentle reasoning and persuasion on my part went out the window. The client told me to get off my high horse as he was paying the bills, and he wanted his wife to be happy. Else, he would take his business elsewhere. So this is the message I relayed back to the creative team, who of course said that perhaps I was not convincing enough! It was like being caught in the crossfire. We gave in. There was no point digging our heels in – especially when what we dug our heels into was quicksand.

This was nothing really – the clients could get quite unreasonable. One of them had scheduled an ad to be released in a magazine. However, he changed his mind at the last minute, and called our Media Manager to tell him to cancel the ad. My manager replied that it was too late as the issue was already printed and would hit the stands in a day or two. On hearing this, he flared up and said, 'Do you know who I am? The ad has to be cancelled at any cost!' and hung up the phone. The manager was flummoxed. If it was Ramana Maharshi – the grand sage of Advaita – at the other end of the line instead of the manager, he would perhaps have replied, 'I do know who *you* are, but more importantly, do you?'

Over time, many incidents like this revealed to me how egoic the profession could be. And there were egos of all shapes and sizes to deal with – something that the advertising industry is notorious for. The creative team were of the opinion that the client servicing team had bigger egos, and the client servicing team felt the creative team could not put a lid on theirs. Of course, they both agreed that the clients had the biggest egos – especially the clients' wives!

It was quite amusing to witness the frustrations that would arise among staff members and with clients. It was a service-driven, deadline oriented profession, and hence a breeding ground for frustration. Everyone was on the edge all the time, and that's even when they weren't. As one of my former colleagues mentioned in a joking yet sombre tone at a recently held reunion that we had, '…and Gautam, on top of dealing with everyone's quirks, whims and fancies, and all the deadlines and late nights, we were selling products to people that they most likely did not need! How could we go to our deaths with that? How could we go to our deaths trying to convince someone to buy the brand of toothpaste advertised by us, and not the others?!' Now he's the Creative Director in one of the largest ad agencies – a tremendous growth curve not only in his career but also his spiritual evolution, I am sure.

Another downer was when we had clients who would not pay up on time, and we had to work up a sweat to collect money that was rightfully ours. I remember one particular instance when a client owed us a lot of money. Repeated calls by our accounts department as well as the senior executives were to no avail, and their pleas fell on deaf ears. The client would even dodge my calls. So, one day, I decided to visit their office. When I reached there, I told the secretary that the purpose of my visit was to collect what was rightfully our due, and I would sit there in their reception till I received the cheque. To show that I was serious, I took along the fattest Robert Ludlum book I could lay my hands on. Till then, I had not been exposed to Nisargadatta Maharaj's teachings else I would have taken my copy of *I Am That*, and then they would have realised I meant it very seriously.

The strategy of a silent protest worked. After cooling my heels for about three hours each over two trips, someone approached me and said there was no need for me to keep sitting there, and my cheque would be given in a week's time, which it thankfully was. Mahatma Gandhi would have been proud. And, perhaps, Ludlum!

And so, while advertising was giving an adrenaline rush, the charm of it gradually started fading away. One does not realise how far away one has drifted, until one has reached the deep end. And then, one realises that one can't go back even if one wanted to. Sometimes, the tide just doesn't turn. It is now clear to me that whatever

I needed to learn during my time in advertising was coming to a completion, and the events that were to follow proved that.

## The waters of publishing

Amidst this scenario came the decision to publish my mother's first book. It was about her experiences in meditation. She was not really interested in the subject. One day, a friend of hers insisted that she visit a guru who was giving talks in the neighbourhood. She was reluctant to attend but went along anyway.

It was as if a dam had burst forth. Back home, she would sit in meditations and get visions of the entire process of Kundalini* awakening, which she would then sketch immediately upon coming out of the meditation, lest she forget them. She is not a trained artist, and yet the results were quite surprising with their consistency in form.

What took shape was a diary with illustrations in colour. She had no intention to get it published, but some friends who were familiar with the subject of Kundalini meditation said that her drawings would be of tremendous value to aspirants on the path. For, it was the first time that the process of Kundalini unfoldment was illustrated so thoroughly, though there were many books that were written on the subject. In fact, in his review of the book, Baba Gagangiri – a revered sage of Maharashtra, referred to it as a 'rarest of rare' occurrence in the physical world.**

---

\*    The manifestation of the Dynamic Female Cosmic Energy within the individual body, lying nascent in a coiled form at the base of the spine.

\*\*   *Conscious Flight Into The Empyrean* – Santosh Sachdeva, Yogi Impressions.

We sent the manuscript to a few publishers and some of them offered to publish it provided we put the money up, as it was expensive to publish colour books. We gave it a serious thought and I felt there was no point in this approach. We might as well publish it ourselves, as that way we could control the creative, design and layout, and make the book look exactly the way we wanted it to. The rationale behind it was that my background in advertising had already familiarised me with the process of design and printing.

It was a decision bold enough to take thanks to that one underestimated quality – ignorance! The designing was the fun part; the printing fairly simple also. However, though we were thrilled with the end result, we realised much later that there was perhaps a better way to have undertaken the project. For, we spent far more than we should have out of sheer lack of knowledge, on the book printing process. What's more, the distributors did not give us the time of day as we had only one title to our credit. One of them actually said to me, 'Come back when you have a hundred titles.' 'That's encouraging,' I thought. We sold books to some stores directly, and never received money for the books even though they had sold the copies sent to them on consignment.

That was how our first book came to be published and got out into the world. Without really getting out, that is. But looking at it from another perspective we learnt a lot from just our first book, which perhaps made it simpler as we went along. There truly are no mistakes. One thing leads to another, and therefore branding it a 'mistake' is just a judgement label we stick onto an outcome.

On a lighter note, it reminds me of the saying, 'Experience is a wonderful thing. It enables you to recognise a mistake every time you repeat it!'

It was clear to me that for publishing to have happened, advertising had to have happened. For, without that background and support, I would not have taken the leap into publishing. As my teacher said: it's not a case of A leads to B, B leads to C... but rather that for C to happen, B had to happen, and for B to happen, A had to happen.

I remember the time when we had to choose a name and logo for the publishing company. As most of my mother's illustrations involved a seated figure in meditation, we created a simple black and white rendering of it, which became our mascot 'yogi'. And, we simply added the word 'Yogi' to 'Impressions' (which was the name of the ad agency). Lo and behold, we had 'Yogi Impressions'. A clumsy name perhaps, but people by and large liked it and so it stuck.

This was how we stumbled upon book publishing. A friend asked me at the time, 'Why the hell did you get into publishing? There is no money in it. You are making a big mistake.' My honest reply was, 'I didn't. It just happened this way.' It reminds me of the time when a leading newspaper had called me a couple of years later as they were doing a feature on spiritual business. The reporter wanted to conduct a telephone interview with me, and asked me what my business plan was. I replied, 'God only knows.' He thought I was joking. When I once again mentioned that I was serious that I did not have a business plan and it was God directing everything, he said that the interview would go nowhere and, thanking me, promptly hung up the phone. Clearly, I wasn't tactful enough.

## God's business plan

Once our first book was out, two synchronistic events transpired. My sister Nikki had recently met Eckhart Tolle, author of the best-selling title *The Power of Now*. She and her group of friends in Hong Kong had been deeply impacted by his book that had just been published in Canada. She expressed her wish to share his message with the people of India. I was sceptical. Our experience with publishing had not been a pleasant one so far. I informed Nikki that while I would be happy to help, she would have to bear the costs of printing the book – something that she was more than willing to. Her intent was that even if it benefited only one person it would be worth it.

Eckhart had mentioned to Nikki that the rights had just been licensed to a US company, and that we should get in touch with them. When we did, we were informed that it was too late as they had just licensed the Commonwealth rights. My sister was dejected. It was not because *The Power of Now* had become a best-seller, for at that point of time it wasn't. It was just that she loved his teaching and wanted to bring it to India as soon as possible. Then what seems a miracle, took place. The US publisher wrote back to say that for some reason, India was not included in the list of Commonwealth countries, and the rights were available. And so, we found ourselves publishing the book. Even today, much gratitude arises for Marc Allen, the founder of New World Library, for placing his trust in our publishing start-up.

It was around the same time that I had started visiting Ramesh Balsekar, a modern-day Advaita sage who lived in South Mumbai. I remember waiting below his building, like everyone else, before the start of his talks. We all had to, till the appointed time when we would trudge up the stairs. One morning his then editor Susie met me below and asked me what I did, and I mentioned my recent foray into publishing to her. The next thing I knew, I was given a call a couple of days later and asked to meet with her and Ramesh over a cup of tea at Ramesh's residence.

When I met Ramesh, he and Susie informed me of a book that they were working on, which Ramesh considered the pinnacle of his teaching. It was *The Ultimate Understanding*. Ramesh had dedicated it to Wei Wu Wei – a 20th century Taoist philosopher of Irish origin – whom he was inspired by. Ramesh wanted this book to be something to cherish – hardbound, art paper... the works. I mentioned to him that I would love to work on it, though the risk would be all his, in the sense that although I had an advertising background I had very little experience in publishing. What's more, money would need to be initially raised for the venture, which could be repaid upon book sales.

He said that was fine, and then asked me which books of his I had read. I froze. I had read none of his books thus far, even though I had been attending his talks on Sundays for the last few months. I was wondering whether to fumble my way through and tell him I had read a bit here and there, or be honest and tell him, 'none'. That word is precisely what came out of my mouth. He burst out laughing and said, 'Then you're perfect for the job.'

What a sense of relief came over me! It was years later that I knew what he meant – in the sense that I was not someone conditioned with his teaching, as that itself could be a stumbling block.

Working with Ramesh on the book was quite an experience. I had hired one of the best-known Creative Directors in the advertising industry at the time, to develop some page layouts to show Ramesh. I was quite happy with the result but when these were presented to Ramesh, I was in for an unpleasant surprise. He did not like the designs, and felt they were not in sync with the contents of the book. I protested, 'But I have got you the best. If you are not happy with it, then you will not be happy with any other Creative Director's work!' And he replied, 'Then you do it.' I was not really a qualified designer and told him that, but it was the end of the matter as far as he was concerned.

And so while I worked on the layouts, a wonderful man by the name of Clark provided the beautiful photographs in the book and Susie was in charge of editing. We all worked as a team and gave our inputs on the final design, including the same Creative Director whose work Ramesh did not like! And, of course, Ramesh loved putting a creative comment in, here and there. It all worked out, eventually.

And so, with books of my mother, Ramesh and Eckhart, I now donned the hat of a spiritual publisher. It's really strange. I had no desire to be in advertising, yet it was my destiny as my father had founded an ad agency. I had no desire to be in publishing, that too niche publishing. Yet, it happened. If my mother had not had her experiences, then the thought of publishing would not have arisen. And for her to have her experiences, she had to be invited by a friend to attend a talk being given in the neighbourhood by a guru. So do I hold the guru responsible for my being in publishing, or his parents, or their parents? Where does this end, or rather, where does this begin? Who exactly do we hold accountable for us being where we are today? The answer is, obviously, no one except God. The Source. Consciousness. I felt like a pawn on a chessboard, being moved by a higher force. It was clear to me that very little was really in my control. In both instances, I was the most unlikely of CEOs, yet I was placed there. I was terrible with numbers, yet had to sign balance sheets. I was an introvert, yet had to deal with people all of the time. Sometimes the Divine plan can seem like a comedy of errors. From our limited perspective, of course.

## Learnings in spirituality

Being in the position of heading a spiritual publishing house gave me tremendous insights into the 'goings-on' of the spiritual community, especially in India. Soon, I became the friend and confidant of devotees and disciples of various teachers, without asking to be one. I invariably came across people happily criticising gurus (besides theirs, of course), and even some gurus criticising other gurus. We're all human, after all. How different was it from the scenario in advertising, I wondered? Invariably, the devotees of gurus with smaller followings had much to say about those with larger followings. Jealousy and envy are perhaps even more pandemic in spiritual circles.

I remember one instance where there were a few of us gathered at a table, and one member of the group kept going on and on about a very popular guru's 'flaws'. The berating seemed endless – it was a monologue. After a while, I mentioned to her that in spite of all that, his organisation had provided water to over 300 villages in India, and I wondered aloud what people like she and me had done to help the cause of the needy. It was quite a silly thing to say but I really didn't know what else would make her stop, and it did stop her from rambling on. She was taken aback. She got her wits together and then went on and on about why I should not have said what I did, for it was comparing apples to oranges.

From then on, I found such opinions and criticisms quite amusing. In they went through one ear and out the other. If I took them to heart, then perhaps most of the gurus, masters and teachers would have dropped off the list, not having made the grade. Heaping on judgements is human nature after all, and one of our greatest indulgences. Thinking of ourselves as the subject and the 'other' as the object, we pronounce judgement upon the object. This was the original sin indeed – usurping the subjectivity of the Source, without realising that we ourselves are also objects in the manifestation.

Another incident that comes to mind is when a yoga teacher casually mentioned that she had seen the aura of one of India's most popular gurus and felt 'it was surprisingly quite insignificant' as it extended just a few inches from his body. She had completely disregarded the fact that there might have been something lacking in her ability to read auras! Of course, her guru's aura stretched over a mile. In any case, all this talk of auras was about yet another phenomenon in phenomenality, and therefore subject to a lot of interpretation. These matters were not of much interest to the teachers of Advaita, and as they were my biggest influence, I took after them. Irrespective of the size of auras and other such things, what mattered to me was the sense of peace that one felt in the presence of an enlightened being. That was truly the only measurable yardstick to go by.

When a large spiritual organisation recently split right down the middle, I got calls from devotees close to both sides, and heard two different positions on what had happened. The guru was left on one side and his seniormost members had walked out to start their own organisation. Both sides put forth their rationale, and wondered what I felt about the situation. For whatever it was worth, I said to both factions that if I saw it from their perspective, they were right; the obvious conclusion when one sees things from the other's perspective. A benefit of this was that everyone was happy about my so-called opinion on the matter. But I did add that, based on my experience, I had seen that nobody was indispensable, and organisations tended to carry on no matter who left. If they were meant to, that is. In this case, I was proved right.

Then, of course, there were the gurus themselves. I have been fortunate to have had close encounters and associations with quite a few of them. I didn't really seek out these meetings, but would not turn any down should an invitation arise. I have really enjoyed being in their company and gained much, especially when I got to see their human side.

Some couldn't help taking digs at others in quite unsavoury ways – yet another testament to the fact that we all have our likes, dislikes and preferences. I even had a situation where a guru criticised my guru while he spoke to me. I found myself smiling right through the criticism and realised that the teaching that 'all there is, is Consciousness and we are all instruments through whom the same Consciousness functions', had perhaps permeated the depths of my being over the years. I still like hanging out with this guru – sometimes maya can be fun!

I have been faced with the situation on a few occasions, when a disciple feels let down by his or her guru and doesn't know what to do. I am asked to give advice on the matter. None is ventured unless asked for. Here I firmly adhere to my guru's tenet, 'Give advice only when someone asks for it.' I find myself saying, 'Why shoot the messenger as well as the message? Take what you got, what impacted your daily living, and stay with it. The rest is just a judgement based on our limited world view, shaped by our conditioning from the day we were born.' We can't help judging actions by some people as good or bad, especially gurus. We build fancy pedestals on which we place them, and then pull them down. In a lot of cases, genuine gurus did not ask to be placed on the pedestals in the first instance.

It reminds me of an uncanny experience I had in a pilgrim town I visit once a year. An author invited me to spend half the day with her, and took me along with some of my friends to a local temple. As with most Indian temples, there were beggars all around. The general tendency is either to give some money or to say something to the effect of, 'I don't have money... Don't bother me...' or simply ignore the approaching beggar. We all would react based on our nature; some would be polite and some would perhaps be rude. However, what I observed was something quite extraordinary. The author pulled out a stick from her bag that became twice its size on being unfolded, held it threateningly at a poor old man approaching us for alms, and said, 'If you come near me I will beat you! Stay away!' Her voice was threatening; her look menacing. I was taken aback. Then, she looked at me and provided the explanation that if you didn't speak to them in this language, they would come after you and bother you... this was the only way. Soon, there was a beggar to the left, one to the right, another behind... and this lady was brandishing her stick. The situation could have got out of hand any moment. I did tell her that this was not really required, but she would have none of it. Did I feel terrible about what was happening? I certainly did. Did I feel compassion? It certainly arose. But more so for her than for them. For, she had authored a book on the subject of being 'one' with all of creation.

But at the end of it all, the realisation was that she too was *being lived* by the Source to be the way she was; a product of her conditioning and genes. It could only be God's will that someone who wrote a book on this subject could be so disconnected, separate and fearful of the 'other'. Yet, my suggestion to someone who read her book and was deeply impacted by it would be the same: why shoot the message?

## Spiritual friendships

Besides devotees and gurus, I am glad my path crossed that of some of the readers of our books. In fact, some became endearing friends over the years. One such encounter left a deep impact on me. A few years ago, we had a run-in with an Income Tax officer. Our books of accounts were a bit muddled as we had to 'rob Peter to pay Paul'. What we used to do was pull in monies from our marketing-related business in order to fund the publishing business in its early years. This left a trail of transactions. We got a notice to report to the authority, and had to end up paying a large amount, close to USD 9,000, as 'miscellaneous expenses' to get out of this sticky situation, else the payout would be higher. I thought we should plead our case as our intentions were good, but my auditor thought that was a preposterous idea and promptly shot it down. We did have the option to protest officially, but that would entail endless agonising months that most likely would lead to nowhere at the end of it all.

A couple of years after this incident, my auditor called to tell me that an Income Tax officer wanted to meet me. 'Oh no, here we go again,' I thought. This time, we had really done no wrong, and I was prepared to put my gloves on to meet the challenge should there be an unreasonable position taken against us. I had no intention of visiting the officer's office, and asked the auditor to represent me. To my surprise, the officer was insistent on only meeting me. This is not normally the case as they are usually satisfied with meeting the auditors of the company. I kept delaying and thought it best that the issue be discussed at their level. I was no good at such discussions and negotiations, and anything to do with book keeping. However, to my utter surprise I was given a call by my auditor to state that if I could not make it, then the officer would come to visit me at my office.

This was not usually heard of, and I thought we were in serious trouble. Income Tax officers didn't generally go around visiting offices. He promptly visited us after a few days. What was the purpose of his visit? He revealed that he had read most of the books published by us and was a fan. God works in mysterious ways, indeed. He then went on to narrate how he came onto the spiritual path, and I was moved tremendously. As is often the case, it usually takes a tragedy or setback to start walking on this path. In his case, it was a life-threatening illness. I also remember him telling me that he wanted to lead the 'quietest existence', and wanted his life to be 'nothing more than a comma'. And I remember thinking that if it was the other officer in his place, his life was already a few commas with many zeros in between!

Here it was – both extremes existing side by side, as exemplified by Income Tax officers. It reminds me of a time at Ramesh's talks, when the two chairs on which one could sit and ask questions to him were taken by two men from different parts of the world, and both their names were Gabriel. Ramesh said something on the lines of: 'Look at the duality as we know it – good and bad, ugly and beautiful, poor and rich, a white Gabriel and a black Gabriel!'

**The end is the beginning**
As the years rolled by, a few setbacks ensured the

advertising ship ran aground. When something is destined to end, then end it must. Our General Manager walked away leaving a staggering debt of over USD 40,000 behind, thanks to one of the clients he had brought in. On top of that, he had been trading on the side with sensitive databases that were part of our direct mailing activity. We discovered this by chance (if there is such a thing), when his laptop came back from repairs and he wasn't in the office on that day. Suddenly, mails after mails of his unofficial dealings were read by a staff member while he was testing the laptop, and the mischief he was up to was bared.

Coupled with this was another substantial monetary loss. We were fighting a case on our tenanted office. We had been there for decades. The landlord had filed a case against us many years ago, stating that as we had converted from a proprietorship to a private limited company, it meant the original owners (my mother and me) were no longer the sole owners although we still retained 75% shareholding. It was decided to give shares to the key members of the team, as they were the ones responsible for running the show. Little did we know this would work against us from a legal angle, as far as the property was concerned. The case went all the way up from the small causes court to the Supreme Court, and we lost it as the court ultimately held that a private limited company was a separate legal entity. On top of it all, you can well imagine the payout in terms of lawyers' fees!

With such events that were entirely beyond one's control, and the funds that got drained out, it was clear that this particular horse had run its race and was now being put to rest.

Thus it was clearly seen that there were far greater forces at work, moulding the so-called future. The money we earned went in meeting these situations. It was clear to me that when money had to go out of one's hands, it simply had to. The rest was just the mechanism of how it went out. We contemplated filing a case on the defaulting client as well as the manager, but my chief accountant at the time was convinced the money would come without resorting to legal measures, which of course it didn't. In any case, it would have taken another 15 years in the Indian courts, and that itself presented such a gloomy picture that we lost interest in pursuing this option. What's more, I really was not the personality type to fight such battles. I just didn't have it in me. You can imagine my relief when I read this extract from *Silence of the Heart* by Robert Adams, a direct disciple of Ramana Maharshi, which thankfully supported my position:

*'The correct way to observe this is to look at everything in the world intelligently without any comments, without any reactions. Do not be for or against anything. Train yourself to observe, to watch, to look without any reaction. You may start training yourself with the small things. Work on the small things first. As an example, if you go outside and you have a ticket on your car for over-parking, catch yourself reacting to this by not reacting at all. Simply see the situation, look at the situation, have no comment, no reaction. Pay the ticket and forget it. Do not think this is good, this is bad, this is outrageous, this is wrong, I don't deserve it. If you didn't deserve it, it wouldn't happen. Say you stub your toe. Instead of cursing the chair, getting upset, feel the pain, observe it, watch it, and let it go. Everything that takes*

*place in your life, this is the way you should react. Someone cheats you, and you're thinking of taking them to court to sue them. Think about this carefully. Is that what I really want to do? And then your ego will say, of course you do, you were cheated. Your business partner cheated you out of $50,000. So you want to take this person to court to sue them. Say you did go to court and you won the case. You think this is good. But something will happen to even it out again. You'll have to go to court again and again and again. Sometimes you will win, sometimes you will lose. There are people like that you know. I'm thinking of a particular woman right now who makes a habit of going to court at least once a month. She is always suing somebody for something. Sometimes she wins and sometimes she loses, and she's a nervous wreck. She is not a happy woman.'\**

Given the ups and downs witnessed in the advertising business, concern would arise regarding the welfare of the spiritual publishing business. In fact, running this business was more difficult as it was not quite a profitable one in any case. It wasn't an easy ride and had its own set of challenges. Yet, I found that when concern for its welfare would arise, so would the thought: 'I did not start it in the first instance. Therefore, let the force that brought this about take it wherever it is supposed to go, or not.' What a relief this thought was! And that's truly applicable to all areas of life. All we can do is what we think and feel that we should; the rest is not in our control.

Facing these big challenges made the transient nature of business very apparent. As I read in an inner chamber course in Tibetan breathing exercises and meditations that

---

\* *Silence of the Heart* – Robert Adams, Yogi Impressions (Indian edition).

I had studied: 'A good supply of resignation is of the utmost importance in providing for the journey of life.' However, the challenges came and went as well, just like the good times. I still found myself sitting at my desk every morning. In spite of it all, the show continued. And with it, the insight that 'this too shall pass'.

Behind me is a picture window that offers a splendid view of the sea from the 17th floor of my corner office. All one can see is the sea, sky and the sun as it marches across the sky from noon till sunset. I turn my chair around and then see this impersonal beauty of nature's grandeur. Nothing really matters to it, forever remaining unstained and unaffected by the individual stories of the billions of 'me's that inhabit the planet, leave alone the 30 or so in our office. And with just a 180 degree swivel of my chair, I am thrown back into the 'working world' and all it entails: the office, the staff and my beloved shrine – the desk. Nature is always there to turn to when one finds oneself entangled in the web of a rough day at work.

**All in a day's work**

My teacher always encouraged people to work. If they were not inclined to, then he would suggest they take up something like social service. However, he did know that deep down if someone was not destined to have a 'working life', then that too was the Divine will in operation. He had this concept of the 'working mind' and 'thinking mind', which I found extremely beneficial. The working mind was always engaged in the moment, focusing on the task at hand. An idle mind can truly be a devil's workshop, which is the 'thinking mind' that is living in the dead past or projecting into an imaginary future, creating innumerable 'what ifs' and 'what should be's' while totally oblivious to 'what is', here and now. The 'me' is held in abeyance when the working mind is in operation as one is totally engrossed in the task at hand. The thinking mind is the 'me', the ego with its sense of separation and doership, and the 'me' comes to the fore when the thinking mind is in operation.

I can truly see that it really helped that my working mind was engaged through those formative years, else I perhaps could have slipped into some sort of despair as the mind would have had ample time to be incessantly engaged in thinking.

As time passed on and the years rolled by, I could see a difference in my attitude to situations that I faced and thus knew that the Understanding had sunk in deeper and deeper. At work, sometimes the same situation tends to repeat itself. This is actually a gift, for one can see if one's attitude has changed in the same context.

One can take it as a deepening of the Understanding if one notices the following:

### Tolerance towards others for their actions

I came to accept that everyone's actions are based on their conditioning and innate nature. There was acceptance of the 'obnoxious' client, or a member of the staff who was not performing as he should. People's limitations (as far as their work abilities are concerned) are seen in a separate light from who they are. It is only then that the issue is addressed, and not the person as such. This approach shifts perspectives dramatically as one takes a more objective view. It does not mean being walked all over by clients, or accepting under-performance by the staff. As in any business, rational decisions based on finance and productivity needed to be taken, but these decisions were no longer directed at 'individuals' but at their abilities in the context of work. Hence, there was no 'sting' directed at an individual in a personal manner.

On another note, I knew that it was my destiny to be cheated of large sums of money, and the 'how' and 'who did it' were just the mechanism of it. This leads to a tremendous degree of tolerance, which in other words is the acceptance of people's actions and the consequences thereof. 'Tolerance' does not imply putting up with others, but rather a tolerance for their so-called 'flaws', just as we too have our own flaws. The focus shifts onto how to handle the present circumstances without getting mired in blame, condemnation and other mental distractions.

### Acceptance of 'what is'

A particular government body had filed a case against all advertising agencies, saying that they now fell within the ambit of this body and were liable to pay some dues. The members of the Advertising Agencies Association were informed not to submit to this but to fight the case in their individual capacities. Of course, the agencies lost. The problem was that when it was time to pay up, we did not have money to pay the dues which were now substantial, with interest add-ons. This was because the case was filed many years ago, even before the time I had joined work. Hence, we appealed the decision and the case dragged on for years, till we eventually lost in the higher court and had to clear the dues. However, the problem was that this body was not informing us as to what exactly was the amount payable upon losing the case. It involved calculations over years, including interest burdens and so on. And, the people at their end in charge of these calculations were invariably on leave. Even eight months after losing the case and getting the judgement against us, we were not able to pay simply because they were not coming up with the amount. This concerned me as it could have meant another few years before they informed us of the amount, and then they would perhaps charge us interest for those years as well!

The lawyers felt we could file yet another case on some other grounds, and delay the matter indefinitely. I would have none of that as it would mean continuously paying their fees, too! Our consultant was left with the only obvious option. He ended up having to grease palms so that someone in this government body would do the math, and tell us what was due to be paid. Can you imagine – first we lose the case and then this, so that the other party can tell us exactly how much we have lost, just so that we can finish paying it off. India can teach you a lot about acceptance of 'what is' indeed. It became easier to accept things as they came to pass. Here was a classic example that there were no limits to what could come by in one's daily living. A healthy dose of acceptance was the best remedy. Acceptance does not mean taking things lying down, but accepting that the unexpected can certainly come your way. Thereafter, you deal with it to the best of your ability and leave the rest to God, as the outcome is not in your control. Very few happenings on the work front surprise me now. If they do, then the reaction is witnessed as a biological reaction without much of an involvement in such events.

The total acceptance of God's will is the total acceptance of 'what is', in the moment.

## The will of God

My working life proved to me that I was a pawn on the chessboard that was the grand design of life. I did what I thought and felt I should, and thereafter God's will took over. It was clear to me that I had to be wherever I was at a specific moment, and the universe had engineered innumerable events to place me there. If my father had not had an ad agency, I would not have been in advertising. If my mother had not had her experiences in meditation, I would not have been in publishing. It was quite a cosmic joke. All the highs at work, and all the lows, all the events that spiralled out of control, and those that miraculously didn't, all the insane surprises, all the little victories and all the setbacks, hammered into the floorboard on which I stood that which is the foundation of all religions: Thy Will Be Done. Nothing can happen unless it is the will of God!

## A shift from reaction to response

During those early years at work, while just in my mid-20s, I encountered many challenging situations. Considering how raw I was, I sometimes found myself getting upset by the language a client had used in his email, and his tone or implications therein. I swiftly sent off a reply, especially when I felt he was not being fair.

Over time, I saw the futility of this approach. Before sending off an immediate reply, I would draft a reply, save it, read it, and then send it after making alterations wherein I felt some words were unnecessarily adding to the drama of the situation.

Some years ago, I had a peculiar experience. It concerned a modern western sage whose books we publish. His new team was being aggressive and accusatory in the tone of their mails sent to my team. I seldom interfere and let things sort themselves out. However, it was becoming a non-stop barrage of mails coming from them and I decided to intervene when I found their last mail out of line, and my team at a loss as to how to handle the situation. I drafted a mail, and was going to send it off immediately. I stopped myself, and decided I would send it off the next morning. When I arrived at work the next morning and re-read the draft, I was in for a pleasant surprise. I could not even move a comma, leave alone change a word. In fact, I wondered if something should be added! It was clear and concise, and stuck to the facts. It was a pure and simple response rather than a reaction. This was a clear example of what my teacher termed as 'deliverance' – the Understanding functioning in daily living. In other words, this is the Understanding operating 'up-front', and not an intellectual processing of the Understanding in the duration of time. In that sense, the space from which the first draft was written made it a response and not a reaction to the events that were transpiring. And this shift is seen not just in drafting mails, but in all aspects of work.

## The final conclusion

When one has the feeling deep down that 'nothing really matters', then one can take it that the Understanding has settled in. Its gift is a feeling of equanimity. Everything seems like a passing show, for that has been one's experience up until now.

Old businesses collapsed, new ones took their place, people joined, people left, accounts came, accounts went, books that we thought would do well did not, books that we didn't pin big hopes on surprised us... the wheel of fortune kept turning, bringing with it one of the greatest understandings of all. It was the understanding that at the end of the day, nothing really matters, no matter how much it looks like it matters. Literally! For in any case, it all disappears in the blissful peace of deep sleep.

It's 10 am on yet another Monday at work. I sit at my desk, and the thought arises, 'Let's see what the day will bring.' During the course of the day, and whenever I feel like it, I swivel my chair to look at the vast expanse nature has so pricelessly bestowed on me – the endless sky and sea, with the sunlight streaming through the window. That too, at no cost to me, whereas here I am in a 1500 sq. ft. office for which a mini-fortune had been paid, full of desks and chairs and walls and computers. What a dramatic irony – all things transitory and man-made come at a price.

Much has been experienced, learnt and witnessed over the passing years. Gratitude arises for the glorious teaching of Advaita, which presents a whole new way of seeing. Events play themselves out more in a natural course, without the added weight of 'me and my story' (a phrase I owe to Eckhart Tolle) that tends to drag situations through the mud like Achilles dragging Hector's body behind his chariot. There is no added weight of blame, condemnation, hatred, malice, etc. and thoughts like: 'How could he? How dare he? What if?' and so on and so forth, that muddies the clear waters of 'what is'.

The feeling is one of lightness and equanimity, swimming with the current rather than against it.

With this arises the deep understanding that the show will go on till it is supposed to. And how long will that be? It's like a dreamed character in a dream asking how long the dream will go on for. Of course, it will go on till it is supposed to, until one awakens from the dream. But, it is not the dreamed character that wakes up from the dream. The dream character dissolves along with the dream when waking up 'happens'.

An appreciation:

*Long after he left the organisation, this touching appreciation came from a former colleague, Husain Agarwala. Perhaps through his keen observation, he witnessed and absorbed aspects of the teaching operating 'in action' during his working hours.*

'Hello and good afternoon Sir,

I just happened to go through your website and a video of your talk. It was amazing to see that you have actually started giving spiritual talks, which I think can influence an individual's perspective on life.

I wasn't really surprised, because I personally was so influenced by the way you talked, you walked, you smiled. Indeed, all the basic thoughts you shared had a deep impact on me and (it) still remains.

I wish you all great luck and God bless you for the spiritual way of living that you have chosen. May the Almighty help you for all the good you are giving to this world and to mankind.

It was a great honour and privilege to work with you.'

– Husain
Mumbai, April 2015

# FORMS OF THE FORMLESS

While sitting at my office desk one morning, I got a call from a close friend. She had been instrumental in encouraging my mother to publish the drawings that depicted, over the years, her spiritual awakening. We became friends during the process of working together on this book as she was actively involved in its conceptualisation and editing. Well-versed in astrology and the healing arts, Ma Amodini Saraswati now lives in Rishikesh and mentors seekers on the spiritual path.

She was calling me to say that she had received a message for me that I should connect with 'Master Kuthumi'. 'Who was the messenger?' I asked. 'Kuthumi himself,' she replied.

I said that I had no idea how I was supposed to connect with him. So rather than sending me a message to connect with him, it would be easier for him to connect with me! This was suggested, of course, in jest. During the course of our conversation I mentioned that I would be travelling to Kashmir in a week. She said, 'No wonder! The timing of the message is perfect! That is where you will get the message. Kuthumi is in Kashmir!'

Now, I had heard names of some of the 'Ascended Masters' of Theosophy but beyond that I didn't know much at all. I turned to the all-knowing, all-pervading Google God and, to my pleasant surprise, found that Master Kuthumi supposedly resided in an etheric realm just above Srinagar's Dal Lake.

Now call it coincidence or part of the Divine plan, it so happened that on my earlier trips to the Valley, I had become quite familiar with and grown to love that particular lake. I would gaze on it whenever I sat out on the balcony of my room at the hotel, situated at the far end of the Boulevard in Srinagar, on a hill overlooking the lake. It is one of the most breathtaking views of Dal Lake surrounded by the crescent-shaped range of the Zabarvan Mountains.

**Nature's cathedral**

I thought Kuthumi couldn't have chosen a better spot for his 'cathedral of nature' in the etheric realms above the Dal Lake. I remarked to my friend, 'Oh, how convenient! I just have to sit on the balcony, close my eyes, and wait for the message to come.'

Of course, it's seldom that easy.

Master Kuthumi is said to have given his sacred teachings to Madame Blavatsky, which resulted in the establishment of the Theosophical Society in the late 19th century. His name is even mentioned in the Puranas, especially in the Vishnu Purana. The esotericism of Kuthumi became more real when I discovered that, in one of his incarnations, he had lived as Kuthumi Lal Singh in Kashmir in the 19th century. There should have been some chest-thumping when I read that he too was Punjabi (Singh also being a common Punjabi surname), but then I did not consider myself a typical lassi-drinking, whiskey-guzzling Punjabi, though I am sure neither was Kuthumi Lal Singh!

So one morning, I ceremoniously brought my cup of tea out on to the balcony and placed some local Kashmiri cookies next to it to dunk them into the piping-hot chai, while looking at the snow-capped mountain range in the distance, mirrored hazily in the lake below. I closed my eyes for a few minutes and waited to hear a Divine voice stage-whisper to me from the crystal blue sky above. I waited a while longer until I realised my chai was getting cold. I thought it would be better if I just sat there enjoying the view of the lake below, and the cathedral of nature around and above, while taking sips of the fragrant tea. I thanked the master, whom I could neither see nor hear, for bringing me face to face as it were to his etheric abode; even if there was no clear message forthcoming from him.

In a way I was glad the 'cathedral of nature' was formless and not limited to a form, as then one would have made another monument out of it. And we all know what happens to monuments over time. What came to mind were the lyrics of a song by 'The Alan Parsons Project' that went something like: *'What goes up must come down... what must rise must fall... if all things must pass, even a pyramid won't last...'* In any case, the natural beauty of the lake and its environs were compelling enough.

Over several trips to Kashmir in recent years, I could not quite figure out what Kuthumi's message had been for me. But I did meet a few mystics and visited some sacred places and thought that, perhaps, Kuthumi's essence was flowing through them.

## The 'Badshah' of Srinagar

When I visited a friend's crystal shop in Pune and mentioned that I would be travelling to Kashmir in the coming week, he suggested that I visit a 'Pir Baba' whom he considered his guru and who lived in Srinagar. He also regaled me with stories of the miracles performed by this Baba in *baithaks* (gatherings of his followers).

He was known as Hafiz Saheb and had a small shop tucked away in the heart of the market in Srinagar, selling the usual touristy stuff like embroidered purses, clutches, shawls, bags and other knick-knacks. As his shop was en route to our hotel from the airport, we thought we would drop in on the way. We were given the name of a hotel as a landmark but there happened to be two hotels by that name. One was within our sight, so we approached it and stopped the car at the crossroads. I got out of the car to ask a local grocer who pointed to the very next shop and said, *'Badshah idhar bagal mein hain.'* (The Badshah is here only, in the next shop.)

I stepped into the dimly lit shop and saw a rather sprightly, grey-bearded man wearing a Kashmiri cap standing at the opposite end. The moment my eyes rested on him, I felt immediately drawn to his composure and bearing. That visit would mark the beginning of an endearing as well as enduring relationship with the 'great king' – the simplest and humblest man one could come across. No wonder he was the 'Badshah'. As a wise man had said: 'The meek shall inherit the earth.'

## A gift of healing

Hafiz Saheb used to hold his gatherings in a botanical garden on the Dal Lake and there would usually be a crowd of 150-200 people who would come to visit him.

People came with all sorts of problems and ailments and he would dispense herbs and extracts as cures, along with the occasional hard slap on the back or a whack on the legs, which I thought would probably jolt the sickness out of the person. Of course, the impact was not felt at the physical level (hopefully) but at the subtle level, to drive the unwanted guest out of the vibrational field of the ailing person. Sometimes, while all this was happening, he would also recite prayers in a soft voice.

When we asked him when the next gathering was likely to be held, he said it had been a while since the last one and this activity no longer interested him. But Hafiz Saheb said he would take us to the garden the next day. It was no longer open to the general public but they allowed him in with his guests. We could not go in through the main entrance, as then others would object and want to follow as well, so we had to go through a hole in the fence on the other side of the garden. This opening was not really visible to the general public.

We sneaked in and the first thing he did was to visit a grave. He asked me to kneel along with him and said a small prayer. Then, pulling out a fistful of breadcrumbs from his pockets, he scattered them over the grave for the birds to come and feed on them. He had a special equation with birds, as I was to find out later. As we walked around the garden he kept pointing out the various shrubs, herbs and bushes, telling us what kind of ailments they were good for. We then sat down on the grass and his Man Friday poured some hot tea from a flask and served it together with some local bread. What an enjoyable way to spend an afternoon – in a botanical garden on the edge of the lake with the mountains behind, and with a man of God who served us some wonderful, aromatic tea! What I remember distinctly is that the Badshah, when he was speaking something of spiritual import, would not be looking directly into one's eyes but rather at the heart area of the person. It felt as if he was talking directly, and with great intensity, to the heart.

**The birds**

Hafiz Saheb appeared to be a man of just about comfortable means yet he lived like a king. Not for himself, but for others. He said he could not be bothered about how much his shop earned him, but by God's grace he always had the resources to spend Rs. 2,000 (USD 30) a week on birdfeed. He would visit five mosques spread across the city to feed the birds on every weekend.

On one of my visits to Srinagar, I decided to hand him an envelope in which I had placed some money so he could spend it as he pleased. He refused to take it but I urged it on him. I didn't know how else to repay his kindness and show our appreciation of the time he had been spending with us. I had even seen some customers enter his shop and leave without buying anything because he was only devoting his time to us. Exasperated at my persistence, he asked me to visit him the next day and keep a few hours free.

As soon as we reached his shop the following day around noon, he gave his assistants instructions to down the shutters as he was leaving for the day. He came in our car and took us to Hazratbal, which is perhaps not just the biggest but also one of the most beautiful mosques in Srinagar. 'Hazrat' is an appellation for the 'Prophet' and 'bal' means hair. The mosque is reputed to contain an invaluable relic – a hair from the beard of the Prophet.

As we got out of the car, I sensed rather than heard a lot of fluttering that could only have come from above. I looked up at the sky and for a minute couldn't believe what I was seeing! Hundreds of pigeons were circling and descending at a predetermined spot towards which we were heading. Suddenly it struck me that their antennae had picked up on the arrival of Hafiz Saheb and they were flocking towards him, waiting for him to scatter sacks of the grain they loved to eat. Cries of 'Salaam alaikum, Badshah' rang out in greeting, which means 'Peace be unto you', as just about everyone, including the beggars seeking alms, seemed to know and love him. He shook hands with them and showered blessings all around. As we made our way towards the shop selling birdfeed, he told me that he would buy the birdfeed with the money I had given him and we would then feed the birds together. We waited as he got busy talking with some people who had come up to him, and he requested me and my brother-in-law to pick up the birdfeed. I asked the shopkeeper to hand me the bag, and he replied it was right in front of me. I could see no bag. There was just a huge plastic tub, about four feet high, that was full to the brim with birdfeed and had a mug placed in it to scoop out the grain. I had noticed that he would pick up the mug and scoop out the amount of grain a customer asked for. In my case, he had just said, 'Le lo!' meaning 'Take it!' Not knowing what to do I waited, while he looked curiously at me to see when I would pick up the birdfeed lying before me.

I waited for Hafiz Saheb to finish greeting his audience. When he did, he turned around and asked us what were we waiting for and told us to pick up and carry that huge tub of birdfeed. To my mind it appeared to contain the shop's entire weekly stock! No wonder the pigeons were going hysterical, making guttural sounds, impatiently stamping their feet on the floor and flapping their wings – waiting for the shower of grain from the Badshah's hands! We went to the area earmarked by the mosque for scattering the feed around; it took the three of us a good 15 to 20 minutes to empty out the entire tub. The pigeons rushed wherever our fistfuls of grain fell and all you could hear was the 'tuk-tuk-tuk-tuk' of their beaks picking up the grain from the floor. Gazing lovingly upon them, Baba turned to me and said, 'When I die, these winged friends will follow my coffin from my home to my grave.' There was no doubt in my mind about this.

**Love for children**
After feeding the pigeons, we went to the main prayer hall where we sat on the carpet while Hafiz Saheb said his prayers, and then off we went to the next destination. This turned out to be an orphanage. As our car drove in we saw young boys in traditional Kashmiri dress and skull caps on their heads, attending a class that was being conducted in a crumbling ruin. Hearing the voices of strangers among them, they looked up from their books and saw us. Suddenly, their faces were wreathed in smiles… their version of Santa Claus had arrived!

Some tables were quickly organised and Baba now made us bring out the three gunny sacks that had been earlier loaded into the boot of our car. He asked my brother-in-law and me to stand on either side of him while the teachers were told to line up the boys. As the boys stepped forward one by one, we distributed sweaters, gloves, and woollen monkey caps for their heads. I was moved to the core of my being at the generosity of Baba. I looked at him inquiringly and said that surely the money I gave him did not cover the expenses of all this as well! I then understood that he had probably emptied out half his shop to bring succour to the children.

What a giver Badshah was! He gave a lot of his time, even foregoing the Eid celebrations at home, to be with these orphans on one of the holiest days in Islam.

Hafiz Saheb turned to me and said, 'Some years ago, I had told my children that our respective families have one another and I was not really needed at such times, so I would instead go to others who don't have anyone in their lives.' Eid was the time for giving and so he gave of himself and his largesse to others. Once a month, he would hire a bus and take some girl students out on a day picnic, which was the only entertainment in their lives. The principal was overwhelmed the first time he offered this and, thereafter, it became a regular feature much to the delight of the teachers and the young girls.

The Badshah walked his talk. One of the tenets of a Tibetan course I had practiced was: 'What you give is what you truly possess.' Thus, he possessed more riches than one could ever imagine. He is truly a great king who gives and therefore possesses the greatest treasure of all – Love. Unconditional love. Consciousness giving to Consciousness without expectation of anything in return, which, in other words, is giving to oneself, for truly there is no 'other'.

The sun had begun to set and dusk was enveloping Srinagar in its cloak. We dropped off Badshah at his shop as his house was close to it. As we were saying our goodbyes, two soldiers who were stationed at the crossroads approached us. One of them told Baba that he had a recurring headache. Baba asked him to come the next morning for a remedy. I wondered whether it would be some herbs and extracts, or a whack on his head from Baba's hand. The sun went down on yet another glorious day in Srinagar as his silhouette faded away into the narrow lane.

If only such 'emperors' ruled all our lands!

## The wizard of Aishmuqam

He looked like Gandalf, the wizard from the movie *The Lord of the Rings*. He was supposedly 75 years old. Supposedly, for no one knew his real age as he had looked the same for the last 15 years or so. He was seated on his *gaddi* (a raised seat), taking occasional puffs from the mouth piece attached to the winding pipe of the hookah. His followers were sitting around him on their haunches wearing their traditional Kashmiri 'pheran' and skull caps. They regarded him as their 'Shirdi Sai Baba'. We really didn't look like we belonged there, as this appeared to be a gathering of simple village folk living in a tiny hamlet on the way to Pahalgam from Srinagar. But Khalid Baba rose from his gaddi and came over to give us a warm welcome.

We hardly understood a word of what he had been addressing in the native Kashmiri language to the gathering. In this case there was no real need to – the love and warmth was so palpable that it didn't require understanding of the words being spoken to amplify it.

The hamlet itself was considered a holy place for it was home to the famous shrine of Rozabal Aishmuqam, in a cave atop the hill. The shrine was of the famous Sufi saint Zain-ud-din Wali who lived in the 15th century.

### The faith of a convert

Sheikh Zain-ud-din, known by his Hindu name of Zia Singh before his conversion, was a prince who belonged to the ruling clan of the Rajas of Kishtwar. For me, it was suddenly cool to be a Punjabi in Kashmir – first there was Lal Singh, and now Zia Singh. I was in good company.

Zia Singh, it is said, was suffering from some disease which took a serious turn leaving no possibility for his recovery. Sheikh Nur-ud-din, a Muslim saint, happened to be passing through Kishtwar at that time. Zia's mother, having heard of the miracles he had performed, begged the Sheikh to visit them and pray for her son's recovery. The Sheikh agreed to pray, on the understanding that Zia Singh would meet him in Kashmir after he had fully recovered.

The prayers worked wonders and Zia Singh regained his health. However, both he and his mother failed to keep the promise made to the Sheikh. As a result, Zia's illness reclaimed him and he was confined to the bed. His mother wept by his bedside, day after day, until one night she had a vision in which she promised to fulfil her promise this time around, if her son would recover once again. 'Wasn't she lucky!' I thought, for Sheikh Nur-ud-din to offer and oblige her with a second chance. As soon as he was restored to good health, Zia Singh went to pay his respects to the Sheikh. Legend has it that Sheikh Nur-ud-din advised him to move to the cave at Aishmuqam and meditate there for the rest of his life.

### Revered as a saint

Aishmuqam is said to house the relics of Hazrat Zain-ud-din. These consist of a bow, a wooden loaf of bread, a rosary, a wooden club and a copy of the Koran. It is said that the saint often observed fasts and whenever he felt hungry he licked the wooden loaf of bread to satisfy his appetite.

Hazrat Zain-ud-din passed away in 1448 CE. When his disciples brought the coffin for burial, they were astounded to see it was empty. In desperation, they left the place and during the night one of the disciples saw Hazrat Zain-ud-din Wali in his dream asking him to raise a *dargah* – a mausoleum – at the site where the coffin had been placed. It is this dargah that is in the cave atop the hill.

The first time we met Khalid Baba, he sent us with two guardians to the cave of the Sufi mystic. It was quite a climb. We entered the cave and paid our respects. The view from up there was spectacular. I think there is something ethereal about the views from spiritual shrines that are built on heights. For instance, one such view is from the Cathar castle of Montsegur in France, which is supposedly one of the last resting places of the Holy Grail.

After we came down from the cave of Hazrat Zain-ud-din, we were treated to a lavish spread of cakes, biscuits, breads, and Kashmiri tea that was flavoured with a hint of salt. We then took Khalid Baba's leave and he bade us a fond farewell while walking with us to our car. We knew we would be seeing him again. And see him again we did. What was endearing was that on each successive trip, he became more expressive – his hugs were warm and reached deep, he planted kisses on our foreheads and eyes, and had walnuts and other dry fruits packed for us to take home. Despite what appeared to be a very conservative environment, his embraces and gestures were so spontaneous that I thought surely some of his more orthodox disciples might be intrigued at what exactly they were witnessing.

## The disciple plays the master

But Khalid Baba was not all soft butter. He would give a shouting every now and then to some of those who had come to see him with their problems. We could not understand what he said to them but he would send them packing, after giving them an earful.

Here is a story about Khalid Baba, which I don't know how far is true. It is quite similar to ones that we hear as part of spiritual folklore.

The story goes that Khalid Baba possessed the gift of bestowing bountiful blessings on newly-weds. It so happened that Baba was once called urgently to a neighbouring village as someone there was critically ill. During his absence, a newly-wed couple had come to seek his blessings. As he was not around, one of his trusted lieutenants took it upon himself to bless the couple with the corresponding ritual. When Baba came back and heard about this, he quietly sat on his gaddi, picked up a piece of burning coal from the chillum of his hookah and put it in his mouth. He then picked up another piece of burning coal with the tongs and, turning to look at the lieutenant, told him, 'Since it seems you can do what I can do, and that too without my permission, please go ahead and put this coal into your mouth.' My guess is that the poor fellow never again attempted to bless any married couple.

## In honour of the mystic

The shrine of Zain-ud-din Wali is respected by all communities and they actively participate in its anniversary celebrations. There is no restriction on entry to the shrine which is open to persons of either sex, of any community. As chance would have it, on one of our trips we landed in Aishmuqam in April on the day of the Urs i.e. the anniversary. Baba gave instructions to his followers that we be made to participate in all the festivities. So, we went to the roof of the building and joined them in lighting torches at the end of long wooden staffs. Hundreds of people were climbing up the hill towards the shrine with these torches. It was a surreal sight – one could see many fires glowing on the hillside in the dark of the night, and all of them pointing to the shrine of the Sufi mystic. It was like being transported back in time.

After lighting the torches, the group recited their prayers to Zain-ud-din Wali. Bowing my head, I was listening to the prayers when one of the interpreters standing next to me nudged me and said with a broad grin, 'We are all worshipping someone who was not born a Muslim. Incredible, isn't it?' After the prayers ended, the people started chanting, 'Shah, Shah... Badshah'. We also added our voice to the fervour of the chanting. Who would have thought that in this remote corner of the world, a Sufi mystic, who had died over 600 years ago, would still be venerated with such devotion.

Aishmuqam is truly a mystical place. It is also said to house the 'Staff of Moses' – the Hebrew prophet who, in Islam, is revered as Musa Ali. The village after Aishmuqam, called Pahalgam, translates literally as 'first stop' and is also known as the 'Village of the Shepherd'. Some believe that it was here that Jesus spent the last few years of his life. I have even read somewhere that both Jesus and Moses are said to be buried near Aishmuqam and Pahalgam. Osho mentions that he has visited their graves at this location. It certainly appears to me a more blessed and ethereal setting, as compared to Rozabal Khanyar where Jesus is supposed to be buried – in the hustle and bustle of a busy street of Old Srinagar.

Coming back to Khalid Baba, he truly looked like someone who did not quite belong to this world but to a long-forgotten era; perhaps to the era of Zain-ud-din. He walked with a gentle gait as if he was stepping on clouds. He had an impish smile. Whenever we politely declined his invitation to lunch, thinking we would be imposing an inconvenience, he would say, *'Accha, phir jaao!'* (Ok, then go!). I would feel that maybe he was upset with us, but he would walk us to our car and I could sense the quiver in his heart when he gave a very tight, warm embrace, before waving goodbye. *'Meherbani',* he would say, before we took his leave.

**An eternal bond**

What is it about these encounters with Kashmir's mystics like Khalid Baba and Hafiz Saheb, and a few others we have met? It's hard to put it in words, for hardly any words are exchanged. Nothing they say has much meaning for us because, even if it did, we would hardly understand what they were saying. We had witnessed no miracles being performed, received no predictions for the future, or anything of that kind, in their presence. Anyway, that was never our purpose in meeting with them.

I had been with a spiritual teacher for almost 10 years in Mumbai, who taught me that the greatest miracle of all was peace of mind in daily living. And that is exactly what I felt with them – a deep sense of peace. That and the palpable absence of separation in spite of being in a society and location where a huge wedge has been driven between people belonging to different faiths and communities. In this light, their unconditional love given so freely and generously is something which tugs at the heartstrings.

Today, a pious and pristine land such as this, often referred to as a 'Paradise on Earth' is the centre of much controversy. It reminds me of the Native American saying: 'The earth does not belong to man; man belongs to the earth.'

**The message**

Back in Srinagar from Pahalgam, and now at the end of yet another soul-stirring trip, I am again sitting out on the balcony of my room, high above the Dal Lake. Hot chai and cookies are lying in wait on the table, while I hope for a parting message from Kuthumi. All is silence, which does not necessarily mean there is no message. As Ramana Maharshi said: 'Speech is always less powerful than silence.'

Perhaps, Master Kuthumi has already spoken with me through the 'Badshahs' of Kashmir.

---

Note: In this essay, the names of the two living mystics have been changed for reasons of privacy.

# THE ROAD AS A GUIDE

A few months ago, a couple dropped in to visit me after having read one of my books. The wife was a keen reader of books on spirituality, while the husband was not. Yet, it appeared that the husband was more impacted by *The Buddha's Sword* and it was he who had requested the meeting.

He said that this book had created a significant shift in his perspective and attitude to life. However, his wife said that there was one aspect that seemed to have undergone no change whatsoever. This was in his attitude towards other drivers when he was on the road. If someone was not driving properly (for example, if someone cut into his lane or simply came too close – something that's rather common in India where there isn't much lane discipline), then he would fly off the handle and really 'give it to the other driver'.

Talking of Indian roads brought an amusing incident to mind, which I shared with them. It so happened that our flight from Pune to Mumbai had been cancelled. Three of us who were to take that flight decided to pool in and take a cab to Mumbai, which is about four hours away. When we were in the cab one of the passengers, who was from Germany, said that he had sworn never to sit in a cab again in India after his last experience. He had no option but to ride one again since he had to catch his flight back home that night from Mumbai. The last time he had sat in an Indian cab the driver was apparently driving recklessly, not maintaining any lane discipline on a highway that did not have a divider between outgoing and incoming traffic and, therefore, that made matters worse. The German, in a fit of irritation and after his heart had skipped several beats, asked the cabbie, 'Are you driving on the left side of the road, or the right side of it?' The cabbie grinned broadly and said, 'Yes.' The man was horrified! I mentioned that perhaps the driver, not knowing English, didn't quite get the sarcasm.

Coming back to the couple, the husband said that after giving the driver of the other car an earful, he would then, in his present foul mood, snap at whoever was sitting next to him in the car. So, his question was that if the book and its message had impacted him in so many practical matters in daily living, why hadn't it also affected his behaviour on the road?

A few weeks after their visit, while driving in Mumbai, I saw a heated altercation between the drivers of a car and a taxi. It appeared that the taxi had banged into the car. Both drivers were standing outside their vehicles in the middle of the road, engaged in an angry exchange of words, and appeared ready to come to blows. Traffic was completely disrupted. Some passers-by were asking them to take their argument to one side of the road, but neither of the drivers was listening. A crowd had gathered around and was vicariously enjoying the spectacle. At that instant, I remembered the couple who had recently visited me and thought an investigation of sorts might provide some insights as to why this agitated reactivity takes place when it comes to cars and roads, and what is the underlying cause of such behaviour.

The human body is made up of five *koshas* or sheaths and what is visible – the *annamaya kosha* or food body – is the most gross and dense of these sheaths. This body is considered as 'me' and one is identified with it. Likewise, one could consider the car one is driving as yet another sheath around us – an extension of ourselves. And so, we are identified with this sheath too. The car is 'my car' just like this is 'my body' as opposed to any other car on the road. In other words, the 'me' derives its sense of self – a sense of who it is – from the car as well. The car becomes an aspect of 'who I am' and if anything happens to the car, my sense of self is diminished because I feel that something has happened to me. And the 'me' does not like to feel diminished. In fact, in many cases, the 'me' aspires to own an expensive car not just for the pleasure of driving it, but for the pleasure of hearing others sing praises of it. This leads to the sense of self, of 'my' importance, becoming enhanced.

The point is that my affectivity depends on the fact that it is 'my car'. If something happens to someone else's car, I might sympathise with his plight, but my sense of self would not get diminished.

To labour the point, why do I fly into a rage when someone on the road inadvertently comes too close to my car, cuts into my lane or, for no fault of mine, dents my vehicle? Simply because it is 'my car' and I am identified with it. It is a threat to what is mine and, therefore, to 'me'. So I want to protect it at all costs. And why do I want to protect it? Because deep down, I am afraid; I don't want to die. In other words, it is the 'me' identified with the body, which does not want to die.

Of course, it is a natural biological instinct to protect oneself. If this wasn't the case, one wouldn't look left and right before crossing the road. Yet, what we see in these instances of losing our cool on the roads is that a natural reaction in the body, when it is threatened in any way on the road, gets converted into a lot of vitriol being spewed in the form of shouting, screaming, blaming, abusing... all sorts of involvement stretching in linear time, rather than just the original, instinctive outburst that happens in the moment.

This reminds me of the example that spiritual teacher Eckhart Tolle gave of seeing two swans who got into a bit of a muddle when they crossed each other's paths in a pond. One of the swans was, perhaps, encroaching on the other's territory. A confrontation took place: they puffed themselves up in a threatening gesture, flapped their wings to show their annoyance and expend their excessive energy, and then glided along their respective paths as if nothing had happened. However, what differentiates us as a species is that we continue to drag the dead weight of an event that was over almost as soon as it happened. The only logical outcome of this is that the weight of it pulls us down, and we sink into the pond.

The point is that we blame others for something they have done to us. Our reaction would be quite different if, let's say, a rock came tumbling down the hillside and hit the side of our car and dented it. There would simply be a focus on what had happened, without blaming and condemning the rock that had rolled down from its resting place. Therefore, it can be seen that we clearly blame the 'other' for something he 'did'. It is this that is at the root of emotional strife.

More often than not, it is seen that there is a series of events and factors that cause such incidents on the roads.

When and where those events had their origin is anybody's guess. And where would the blame-game stop? Besides blaming the 'other', we would have to blame the person who invented the wheel, those who built the roads, those who invented cars, yourself for possessing a car without which the incident would not have happened, the situation at work you were thinking about at the time that made you slightly inattentive and, therefore, resulted in the incident, and so on and so forth. All these factors contributed to the incident happening in that very moment. And all this would apply to the other driver as well. Could it truly be anyone's 'doing' as such?

Who is to blame whom in such a scenario? Ultimately, the incident on the road happened because it was meant to, and not because someone 'did' something even though, on the face of it, it does look like what someone – 'me' or the 'other' – did.

This, of course, does not absolve a person of his responsibility to society, which has laws in place to curb violence. We have all seen reactions taken to the extreme when we view violent incidents of road rage on television. And, thankfully, society has laws for that. But what the actual trigger for such events is, God only knows. Some of these triggers are deep-rooted in conditioning received in the early, formative years of childhood and are based on a conditioning of competition – that of 'me' versus the 'other' and all forms of jealousy, envy, hatred and malice, mired in whirlpools of separation. Unfortunately, the basic Unity of all beings – the Consciousness that binds us together – is relegated to the background, and separation in terms of different bodies fighting for survival – physical and psychological – is brought to the fore.

Many years ago, I was walking towards my parked car. There was a car that had pulled up barely a few inches behind mine. The driver was sitting in the car. He saw me walking up to my car and I saw him looking at me, so I assumed he would back up a bit and give me space to reverse the car so I could exit the parking space. I got into my car, started the ignition, and saw that he did not budge but was simply looking the other way. I honked, but he pretended not to hear. The thought arose, 'Boy! How stupid… is he unable to hear or what?' I got out of my car and in a stern voice said something to the effect of: 'Do you have a problem?' And then I remembered the words of my spiritual teacher Ramesh Balsekar: 'If everything is God's will, why would anyone 'do' anything stupid?' I almost burst into laughter at that thought! The driver then grudgingly reversed the car; I got into mine. I could see him in the rear view mirror, mumbling something and perhaps swearing away, but I happily drove on.

What I was pleasantly surprised to note was how a shift in perspective just dissipates the possibility of any involvement, leaving whatever arises in the moment to just 'be' without stretching it out. So much energy is dissipated in these prolonged bouts of unnecessary involvement; the only consolation being in knowing that even that had to happen. Yet, over time, it is witnessed that the involvement gets lesser and lesser until one looks back, one day, at such an incident and realises one was no longer 'involved'. This is the way of the swan.

Here, yet another incident springs to mind. I was once in a taxi driven by an elderly man. He had unknowingly squeezed past another car too closely and both our vehicles had pulled up next to each other at the signal. This happened near the Gateway of India. The driver of the other car, taking into consideration the taxi driver's age, casually remarked, *'Kyon kaka, kya aap kabutar dekh rahe the?'* (Why, uncle, were you busy watching the pigeons?) To this the taxi driver replied, *'Mein toh kabutar dekh raha tha, lekin tum kya dekh rahe the?'* (I may have been looking at the pigeons, but what is it that you were looking at?) Both drivers then grinned sheepishly at each other and, thankfully, moved on when the light turned green. If only all reactions were laced with some wit and light-heartedness!

Referring to what is 'spiritual awakening', my spiritual teacher made a subtle yet clear distinction between 'awakening' and 'deliverance'. He said: 'Enlightenment is sudden, but deliverance is gradual. The flash of total acceptance that I cannot be the 'doer' of any deed is sudden. Thereafter, living one's daily life with this total sense of non-doership is gradual. It is like learning to drive. Getting the driving license is one thing, but becoming a seasoned driver and driving smoothly through heavy traffic may take some time. Until one day, after a few months, you look back and realise that you have just driven through heavy traffic for over an hour without undergoing the least mental stress.'

And that's where my conversation with the couple had ended. I said to the man that when he looks back and realises that there has been a change in his attitude towards the 'other' on the road, then it is a sign that the teaching has sunk in deeper. What could he do to hasten the process? Nothing! Sometimes, a clear understanding that sheds light on a situation should be left to do its job and arise, when it is supposed to, without the 'me' trying to take ownership of the understanding so it can implement it when it wants to. As is most peoples' experience, this hardly ever works and more often than not such an approach meets with failure.

That's why one has the reaction: 'There I go again, in spite of my best efforts!' That was perhaps the reason why he was not finding a change in his behaviour on the road.

On a lighter note, the business of driving a new car (especially on Indian roads) is a stressful one for many. As we say here in Mumbai, we are simply waiting for the first dent to happen. It's a question of 'when' rather than 'whether' it will happen. And the heart sinks when the first such incident occurs. The degree it impacts us is the degree to which we are identified with the car. And don't most of us identify with new objects, which we acquire in our life, to a great extent?

A friend of mine had recently acquired an expensive luxury car. Shortly thereafter, he noticed that it made a slight rattling noise and in spite of sending it back to the service centre several times, the problem could not be rectified. Because of this, he said that his initial thrill of acquiring the new car had evaporated into thin air. And by the time the garage managed to locate the cause of the rattle and rectify it, it was too late. The damage had already been done – that is, to his feelings about the car.

On the other hand, there is this other friend who has a very practical approach. To save himself the stress of his new car getting dented, and the ensuing heartbreak, he makes the first dent himself – in a place not visible externally. He will take a small nail, scratch the metal on the inside of the curve above the wheel, and then he rests easy. For, he knows the second dent never has such a forceful, emotional impact as the first one; just as when you receive a hard blow early on in life, the subsequent ones don't seem to have that much force behind them. The only difference being that in this case he struck the first blow, a very soft one, on himself!

One wonders if this would really work!

# ASPECTS OF THE MIND
# AND THE ARROWS OF DESTINY

Strongman. Expert marksman. Mountain climber. True patriot. Folk hero. William Tell was all this and more. Legend places him in the early 13th century, in the countryside of Switzerland. Around that time, the emperors of the Habsburg dynasty of Austria were making a bid to dominate Uri, in central Switzerland. Towards this end, the Habsburg emperor appointed Albrecht Gessler as the overlord to rule over Uri from his castle in Altdorf.

A tyrannical ruler, the newly appointed Gessler raised a pole in the village's central square. He hung his hat on top of this pole and demanded that all the townsfolk who passed through the square had to bow to it.

On 18th November 1307, William Tell, visiting Uri along with his young son Walter, passed through the square and walked past Gessler's hat, publicly refusing to bow before it. He was immediately arrested by the guards posted there.

Gessler, who had heard about Tell and his legendary marksmanship with the crossbow, thought of a devious way to punish him for his act of disobedience. He ordered Tell to place an apple on his son's head and split it with an arrow from his crossbow in a single attempt, or else face execution along with his son.

This was a life or death moment for William Tell. The perfect marksman that he was, Tell squared his shoulders, breathed deeply, focused his mind and took aim. He let the arrow fly and neatly sliced the apple without hurting a hair on his son's head.

However, Gessler had noticed that Tell had removed two arrows from his quiver and not just one, even though he had been allowed only a single attempt at the apple. As he was about to release Tell, he asked him why he had removed two arrows instead of just one. Tell replied that if he had by chance killed his son, he would have then used the second arrow to kill Gessler.

Hearing this, Gessler became infuriated. He ordered that William Tell be bound and brought aboard his boat to be taken to his castle, where he would spend the rest of his life in a dark dungeon. As luck would have it, a storm gathered over Lake Lucerne and the sailors could not handle the ship in the seething waters. Afraid that the vessel would capsize and they would all drown, they decided to untie Tell so that he could help them steer it with his famed strength.

Seizing the moment providence offered him, Tell escaped by leaping from the boat at a rocky site (now known as the *Tellsplatte* or 'Tell's slab'). He then ran cross-country to Gessler's castle. Gessler did not know what had transpired on the waters. Tell waited in hiding and as Gessler arrived, he shot him with the second arrow from his crossbow.

William Tell's act of defiance sparked a rebellion and struck the first blow in the Swiss struggle for liberty from the Austrian yoke. In 1315, he fought again in the Battle of Morgarten, which proved to be a decisive victory and paved the way for the formation of the Swiss Confederation.

## The working mind and the thinking mind

My spiritual teacher, Ramesh Balsekar, drew a clear distinction between two aspects of the human mind that we are all familiar with:

1. The 'working mind' that dwells in the 'now' and operates in the moment.
2. The 'thinking mind' that delves into the dead past or projects into an imaginary future, both of which do not exist.

He would give the example of a surgeon who, while performing an operation, is focused fully on the task at hand. At that moment, the surgeon is using his working mind. The thinking mind comes into play if and when his mind starts wandering, and wondering about what could happen if something goes wrong with the operation while he is performing it.

For instance, if the patient being operated upon is an influential politician, the surgeon could start worrying about the consequences he would have to face if something went wrong. He would then be using his thinking mind and getting 'involved', which could distract him from the operation and thus affect the outcome of the surgery.

However, it should be made clear that the working mind would of course dip into past experience to help the surgeon conduct the operation to the best of his abilities.

In short, the thinking mind operates in the realm of 'what if', whereas the working mind operates in the realm of 'what is'.

The story of William Tell seems an appropriate demonstration of this concept. Tell was placed in a critical situation. With a single arrow, he had to slice the apple placed atop a young boy's head and moreover, the boy in question happened to be his own son. It is a classic scenario where the thinking mind might very understandably come rampaging to the foreground. Tell's world would come crashing down if he missed. Yet, in spite of this extreme pressure, he managed to split the apple with his arrow.

Being conditioned as a warrior who had acquired skilled marksmanship with the crossbow, Tell was able to remain completely focused on the task at hand, affixed in the working mind mode. As a result, he was able to shoot the arrow straight through the target. If his mind had been galloping all over the place filled with fear, apprehension and doubt, even a few millimetres off the mark would have proven fatal for his son.

The 'galloping mind' is the thinking mind, the 'me' with all its acrobatics and worries. The working mind and the thinking mind cannot be in operation simultaneously. When the working mind is engaged, the thinking mind – the 'me' – is absent. When, figuratively speaking, there is no 'me', the working mind is operating.

The thinking mind is characterised by 'involvement' in the thinking, which distracts a person from the task at hand. The working mind is characterised by the 'absence of involvement', resulting in 'mindfulness' – being totally present with 'what is' here and now.

William Tell's working mind was functioning in pristine condition, without the strain of any involvement in horizontal thinking, thus enabling him to hit the target with extraordinary precision.

## The arrows of destiny

However, being the cautious man that he was, Tell had factored in the possibility of failure and was fully prepared for his next action in case he missed and ended up killing his son. He did not take it for granted that he would strike the target. Plan B was in place, as part of the functioning of his working mind. The second arrow was ready, and would have been used immediately to kill the tyrannical overlord had things gone wrong.

Yet, how and when the second arrow would be used was not determined by Tell, but by destiny. After all, he had no intention to use the second arrow if the first one hit the mark. He had to have possessed the humility of knowing that in spite of his great skill with the crossbow it was God's will that would actually prevail, but he could hardly have imagined a scenario in which his son would be saved *and* Gessler would be killed! It was clearly destiny which ordained that Tell would be the instrument through which both actions happened.

## The restless mind

A young boy I met recently was quite taken with this concept of the working mind and the thinking mind. He inferred that to prevent the thinking mind from going on a rampage, one should always keep the working mind engaged. This has some truth in it, but only up to a point. The mind can be mischievous – just like he proved with his next statement. He said that he would spend hours every day on video games, therefore keeping his working mind engaged. So he felt happy that he was doing the right thing and his thinking mind was not given free rein, as it had been a source of constant trouble for him.

If one is prone to be taken over by the thinking mind incessantly, then yes, getting involved in an activity that deliberately engages the working mind may be a good alternative. In that sense, an idle mind is truly a devil's workshop. However, at its core, this state of affairs indicates a restless mind, not a mind at peace. A deliberate attempt to engage the mind is in fact a type of involvement itself, and can therefore offer only a short-term solution at best. The restless mind is the monkey mind that needs to keep latching on to something or the other in order to keep itself occupied. But this will only appear to work until, of course, the monkey mind gets exhausted.

In a conversation I had with a lady who had been a spiritual seeker for many years, this predicament was brought to the fore. She mentioned that she no longer had any need to work since she was now financially secure, so she had developed about 15 passions that kept her busy during the day. These were hobbies like painting, listening to music, studying the Bhagavad Gita, etc. With tears in her eyes she said that while this helped her pass the time, she was still not at peace and felt something was 'missing'. It is clear from this example that true peace resides elsewhere, and not in keeping one's working mind occupied through 15 or even 150 passions.

## Disengaging the mind

On those rare occasions when the mind is quiet, the peace and calm of stillness shines through. While taking a walk in nature, watching the sunrise or sunset, or for that matter watching the breath, the mind is disengaged and one is just being with 'what is'. The awareness dawns that there is a state of being apart from that of an engaged mind. And that state of being is 'witnessing'.

Upon some reflection, one sees that keeping the mind constantly engaged is a subtle ploy to camouflage the greatest fear of all – the fear of death. It is akin to wrapping a cloak around the fear of death, for a purposefully engaged mind is a mind that is afraid to die. It is constantly finding ways and means to dodge the question that must inevitably come up sooner or later: *Who am I if I am not my mind? What would happen to 'me' if I was not engaged in some mental activity or another?*

Intentionally keeping the mind engaged all the time is just a means of avoiding these burning questions. But once this is deeply recognised, the inquiry goes within and sincere seeking begins. It is now no longer an external engagement; this time around, it is an internal one. The arrow from the crossbow has been shot within, straight to the heart of the matter. Literally. For it is then realised that when you're not in the mind, you're in the heart. The heart of 'I am'; not the mind of 'I am Gautam'. 'I am' – as the awareness of simply being, of existing. Not existence as a separate entity, or ego.

One may well ask: *Who will I be without my mind?* And that is precisely it! One will simply 'be'. Then, the engaged mind is laid bare. It is stripped naked, for it is clearly seen that the thinking mind is the ego, the separate 'me' that constantly identifies with the activities it engages with in order to derive its apparent existence from them. As stated earlier, it is now clearly seen that the compulsively engaged mind is nothing but a covert attempt at camouflaging the fear of death. Death of the 'me'; death of the 'me and my story'. For without the thinking mind, the 'me and my story' cannot exist.

If you can be by yourself, be with nature or more importantly 'be' no matter where you are, it is a good pointer that you are free of the shackles of the engaged mind. You no longer seek constant shelter in the working mind in order to escape the thinking mind. But, if each minute of your time needs to be spent engaged in some activity or the other, no matter how covert, it is a clear pointer to the grip that the mind still has over just 'being'.

A girl I know once remarked that she had to always be doing something as she just couldn't sit still for a moment. If there was nothing else she could find to do, she would start checking the status updates of her friends on her mobile phone... even if she had checked them just 15 minutes ago! Repeatedly checking on status updates was an obsessive attempt to keep her mind engaged, else she would feel uneasy and restless. Her restlessness was then reflected onto that activity, so it momentarily made her feel that all was well with her world.

Renowned Advaita sage Nisargadatta Maharaj had some pertinent words to say on this matter:

*'It is all a matter of focus. Your mind is focused in the world, mine is focused in reality. It is like the moon in daylight — when the sun shines, the moon is hardly visible.*

*Or, watch how you take your food. As long as it is in your mouth, you are conscious of it; once swallowed, it does not concern you any longer. It would be troublesome to have it constantly in mind until it is eliminated. The mind should be normally in abeyance – incessant activity is a morbid state. The universe works by itself – that I know. What else do I need to know?'*

The mind can even trick one into believing that one is just 'being'. For example, when one is in nature and the process of labelling begins: *That's a beautiful blue sky – I can't quite remember seeing such colours before. I wonder what those lovely, green trees are called...* and so on; everything gets labelled non-verbally by the mind as you take a walk through the park, missing the true essence of the moment. It reminds me of the time when a friend, whom I met over a coffee, went on talking in a monologue for over 30 minutes on how much she loved... silence!

**The dawn of witnessing**

Meditation is often advocated to quieten the mind. However, it is seen that many people find it difficult to sit with closed eyes and just 'be'. To assist them in the process various techniques are prescribed such as: watching the breath, reciting a mantra or even counting the thoughts that come. This often seems to help the individual, depending on his or her predisposition to the particular technique. The idea is to bring them to the witnessing state, where they are no longer identified with

---

* *I Am That – Talks with Sri Nisargadatta Maharaj,* Chetana Publishers, Mumbai, India.

their thoughts and can just witness them in the same way as they might witness something as mundane as traffic going by on a busy street.

However, despite their best efforts this is a state that still eludes a lot of people, the reason being that there is nothing you can really 'do' to be a witness. Why? Because 'doing something' would be engaging the mind, and an active mind simply cannot witness. Witnessing 'happens' when the mind is still. Doing something would be engaging the mind to stop the mind – which is impossible.

One day, at the end of a meditation session, a girl mentioned that she had had a brilliant meditation because she was able to 'concentrate' so hard that there was not a single thought. Something didn't ring quite true and I was left wondering. Either it was not a 'brilliant' meditation, or she was using the incorrect word. The matter was clarified the next time she came, when she reported that her mind had remained blank for three days after that meditation, in stark contrast to its usually restless ways. I then realised that the word 'concentration' was simply an inaccurate way of expressing what had happened. Perhaps out of sheer conditioning we tend to attribute everything to the mind, even stillness. She had clearly had a very deep taste of a truly still mind, and its ramifications were apparent in her experience over the three days that followed the meditation.

I was pleasantly surprised later to come across these words of Ramesh Balsekar, which shed light on the matter:

*'Meditation is often misunderstood as concentration on some word or image, but concentration means excluding*

*everything, rejecting everything. It is a self-centred activity. Meditation really means absolute clarity, which can only come about in the total silence of the mind, not the self-centred concentration. Clarity can only happen when you are not concentrating on something, not when you are excluding everything, but you are merely silently being aware and attentive to every thought, every movement, without trying to correct anything... it is in this awareness, pure awareness, that all thinking and reacting dissolve and leave the mind vacant and open to the moment.'\**

When witnessing is happening, there is no 'you' involved with your individual thinking mind. So 'your' attempt to concentrate in order to stop the thoughts from coming during meditation is futile; even the attempt to be a witness is futile. However, in that very moment when you realise the mind has been involved in thinking you get a true glimpse of witnessing, for 'something' has to realise that one was involved in thinking. That 'something' is the Witness. And that is not a function of the engaged mind. So, it isn't really 'you' who realises that the mind has been involved in thinking, but rather the realisation happens – it dawns – that there was involvement in thinking.

As one goes deeper into meditation, there is naturally less and less involvement with the thoughts that flow through the mind. 'Involvement with thoughts' means becoming engaged in thinking and conceptualising. Thoughts may of course arise in meditation but the rampaging thinking mind does not run away with them

---

\* Ramesh Balsekar quoted in *Calm Is Greater Than Joy* – Shirish Murthy, Zen Publications, Mumbai, India.

into the sunset and over the cliff! They are simply witnessed. It is then seen that 'I am not my thoughts'. This actually means that when there is no involvement in thoughts in the form of further thinking, there is no 'me', and the 'thinking mind' is not operating.

To labour the point: when involvement in thoughts gets spontaneously cut off, witnessing begins. However, you cannot directly cut off the involvement with your thoughts, because 'you' *are* the involvement. The involvement can only get cut off by that which is not 'you' i.e. when witnessing happens.

'I', as a separate 'me', can never witness. I can only observe. For example, a separate 'me' can observe an object or, let's say, another person. And to observe something is to judge it as good or bad, beautiful or ugly and so on, in a subject-object relationship. We, thinking we are the subject, pronounce judgement upon the object. In witnessing, where there is no separate 'me', judging simply cannot arise as there is no 'me' separate from the 'other' to do the judging.

**Witnessing and the working mind**

So, what comes closest to witnessing? It is the working mind, for in the working mind there is no 'me', or in other words, the thinking mind; the ego. When you are in the working mind, you are in the 'I am', and witnessing means being in the 'I am' too.

But it must be clearly understood that the two are different. The working mind is 'I am' in action, and the mind cannot witness, while witnessing only happens when the mind stops working. The boy who constantly engages himself in playing video games is quite clearly keeping his working mind engaged. But what he seeks deep down is the peace of a disengaged mind, the peace of witnessing, the peace that is the absence of both the thinking mind and the working mind. In other words, what he seeks deep down is to get as close to the peace of deep sleep as is possible in the waking state. The peace of deep sleep is peaceful simply because there is no 'me', though one exists. But that peace can't be 'achieved' because it would mean that someone wants to achieve something, whereas witnessing is the very absence of that someone as a result of which the witnessing arises. It's akin to the simple fact that one cannot 'achieve' deep sleep.

The 'I am' is the purest state of meditation. But you can't do anything to be in the 'I am', for in a manner of speaking you already are the 'I am'. You cannot be 'I am Gautam' without being 'I am' – existence, pure and impersonal, without the taint of the ego and its sense of separation. You cannot 'do' meditation, but meditation can *happen* when there is no 'you' attempting to do meditation.

When the engaged or restless mind dies down, the light of witnessing shines forth in all its glory.

### God's will and 'my' will

Seen in another light, the total acceptance of God's will is the total annihilation of 'my' will. The total annihilation of 'my' will is the total annihilation of 'me'. The total annihilation of 'me' ('I am Gautam') is the total presence of 'I am'. The total presence of 'I am' is the blinding light of witnessing.

And what is God's will in operation? This can be clearly seen in the legend of William Tell. Was it a progression of events, or a regression, or both? As Ramesh would say, the arrow of cause and effect is double-pointed. The story is backwards. It seems that A leads to B, and B leads to C; but it is clearly seen that for C to happen, B had to happen; for B to happen, A had to happen. Nisargadatta Maharaj referred to this as 'reversing into the future'.

For Gessler to have died, Tell had to be born. Tell had to have been trained as a huntsman and a warrior. He had to have had a son. Gessler had to have had the thought to put his hat on a pole and demand that people bow before it. Tell had to walk past the hat on the pole and refuse to bow to it. Tell had to possess sufficient humility to keep two arrows ready, in case he failed and ended up killing his son. When questioned by Gessler, he had to have given the answer that he did, which in turn infuriated Gessler. There had to have been a storm on the lake. Tell had to have been able to escape and then wait in hiding to kill Gessler with his second arrow, which he never intended to use if he struck the apple with his first shot and so on and so forth, *ad infinitum*.

It is truly astounding to contemplate the intricate engineering of this set of events involving William Tell that directly impacted the formation of the Swiss Federation. Clearly, Tell and Gessler were but two instruments within the larger scheme of things – the landscape of God's Plan.

Likewise, one can only marvel at the complex synchronicity of the set of events that line our own days, and how the universe conspires to bring about 'what is' in our lives. It is indeed humbling to truly see how there really is so little of 'my will' in the gigantic and sprawling network of events that make up one's daily life. Yet, we glorify this 'my will' as we often fret, fume and stress about things not going our way; the way we want them to. Well, whose way are they going then? But of course, God's Way, which many a time our limited 'thinking mind' cannot comprehend as it doesn't make sense to us. We often realise how exercising 'our will' has gotten us into so much trouble. Yet exercise it we must, as that is the mechanism of functioning in daily living. All we can do is try our best in a given situation, and leave the rest to God.

The sage Ramana Maharshi had the final word on the matter:

*'The Ordainer controls the fate of souls in accordance with their prarabdha karma. Whatever is destined not to happen will not happen, try as you may. Whatever is destined to happen will happen, do what you may to prevent it. This is certain. The best course, therefore, is to remain silent.'* *

Ramana Maharshi, of course, was not referring to us just zipping our lips, but to the true silence of the mind, to inner Stillness.

---

* *The Teachings of Ramana Maharshi* – Sri Ramana Maharshi, Edited by Arthur Osborne, Sri Ramanasramam, Tiruvannamalai, India.

# MAHARAJ AND THE TROJAN HORSE OF CONSCIOUS PRESENCE

Over hundreds of years, in various spiritual traditions and teachings across different cultures, the ego has been portrayed as a villain – the source of all one's troubles. Many of these teachings tell us that the ego must be killed. My spiritual teacher Ramesh Balsekar, however, did not share this view. He used to ask, 'Who is being told to kill the ego? Who else, but the ego! And would the ego ever agree to kill itself?'

To tell the ego to kill itself is akin to 'making the arsonist in charge of the fire engines'.

Ramesh would further elaborate that the ego was a necessity for inter-human relationships to develop, and for life as we know it to happen. His teaching would then proceed with asking the individual, the 'ego', to perform a simple practice that he referred to as self-investigation. In this investigation, one explored whether one's actions were truly one's own actions, or were dependent on a multitude of factors over which one had no control. This aspect of his teaching is covered in most of his books.

Ramesh's guru Nisargadatta Maharaj's approach was quite different. Whenever visitors would ask questions of Maharaj, he would pre-empt them by saying: 'Don't ask questions as one individual to another, but as consciousness to consciousness.' This posed a conundrum for some spiritual seekers. For, what questions would be left if they couldn't ask them from the standpoint of the ego – the individual 'me'? All problems in life are after all related to one's hopes, desires, dreams, fears, failures, and so on. If one was not an 'individual' with one's own personal story, then where would the question of problems arise?

Maharaj's teaching was based on the concept that 'you are not the body'. He would keep telling those who visited him, to turn their attention inward to the animating presence – 'I am'. This 'conscious presence' is that without which one would not 'be'. Without this presence of consciousness, the body would be lifeless.

Ramesh, on the other hand, would say that this 'I am' is the only Truth that no one can deny. For no one can deny that they exist. He would refer to it as an 'impersonal awareness of being'. Impersonal, for if one's entire memory were wiped out, one would yet be aware that one exists. It is this awareness that gets personalised with the advent of the ego when a child reaches the age of 1½ to 2 years. 'I am' is the impersonal presence, and 'I am Gautam' is the ego – identified with a name and form.

To give an example that might make this easier to understand, one can see that this impersonal awareness – the 'I am' – is that which witnesses the march of time as one clocks more birthdays and grows older. 'I am 20; I am 30; I am 40...' Who is this 'I am' that knows these milestones? It is obviously something that is apart from the body, which knows the body is that respective age. In other words, it cannot be its own age, else it would not know it.

As Ramesh, quoting Wei Wu Wei, once said: 'How can we know that the world is transitory, that time is passing, that nothing stands still? We cannot know that the river is flowing unless we have one foot on the bank! There is no entity, only a continuum. And that continuum is Consciousness.'

Maharaj would urge some seekers to 'abide in your beingness'. For those of a simpler mindset who probably would not comprehend that message, he would recommend bhajans and japa. On some occasions, he would even suggest the practice of simple affirmations or reflections.

I chanced upon these affirmations when I started reading Maharaj's books. Somehow the affirmations stood out as they were quite unexpected of Maharaj.

The dictionary defines an affirmation as, 'a positive statement or declaration of the truth or existence of something'. And Maharaj's affirmations were literally just that, for they kept affirming 'the only truth that no one can deny' – 'I am, I exist.' I exist not as a separate individual – 'I am Gautam' – but as That which enables me to say 'I am Gautam'.

In the Tibetan course of breathing exercises that I practised, one of the affirmations was, 'The riddle of the universe is about me, and I am now solving it.' This was astonishingly close to Maharaj's teachings and what he often said: 'Abide in the beingness, the I Amness, and it will reveal its secrets to you.' Maharaj was pointing to That which is even prior to beingness, 'before you were born,' as he would say. To emphasise the point, he would sometimes say, 'What were you a 100 years before you were born?'

But that's quite another matter.

Some may find these affirmations rather simple. However, they are deceptive in their simplicity, as are all the great wisdom teachings. Ramesh would say, 'Always remember, beauty in simplicity.'

I remember the day I went to Ramesh with the manuscript of my first book based on his teaching, which covered its core concepts. It was short and concise; perhaps too short. I wasn't surprised when, after going through it, he remarked that it could have been longer. When I said I could work at it and elaborate on his teaching, he answered, 'No no, simple is good. That's the way the teaching went in, so that's the way it came out!' For a minute I thought he was joking, but he said it in all seriousness. I thought it was 'either that, or he must think I have a very basic level of intellect'. He must have noticed my expression for, with a chuckle, he quickly added, 'If it was thicker, we could have charged more!'

Maharaj's affirmations and reflections are like the Trojan Horse[1]. They come disguised as a wonderful gift for the ego that is stealthily brought within its ramparts. Although disguised as a gift, hidden within are warriors ready to strike at the heart of the ego and its identification with name and form as a separate entity, as distinct from the 'other'. While these affirmations are few and far between in Maharaj's books (and, therefore, his talks), what they all have in common is that Maharaj says with firm conviction that they will 'take you to that state'. Maharaj did not suggest that seekers simply repeat 'I am not the body', even though that was his basic message. He knew only too well that to suggest a negative affirmation (negation) such as 'I am not the body' would not work.

After all, as Ramesh would say, the ego *is* the separate individual, the 'identification with name and form as a separate entity'. Such an affirmation, so to speak, would not really make any headway. It would not penetrate the depths of one's being. The natural programming the ego has been endowed with is that it is very much identified with the body and hard-wired with it – just like the shell on a turtle's back. Therefore, the ego would put up resistance – consciously or unconsciously – to negating itself into oblivion. It would jeopardise the process, for the arsonist would be given charge of the fire engines; the thief would be given charge of the police station.

However, though they are affirmations, they operate as covert negations. What they affirm is the pristine, impersonal sense of presence untouched by the acrobatics of the 'me'. And by doing so, what they negate is the existence of the individual, the 'me', as separate from others. Maharaj was clear that he had to demolish the individual's identification with the body. Instead of pitting the ego against the ego, what Maharaj suggested was affirmations that embraced the ego; affirmations that the ego would have no problem in affirming. This is the approach he took with some seekers.

It's important to note that these affirmations and reflections do not need to be memorised and recited in a punishing routine. It is the ego, the 'thinking mind', that does this in the hope of deriving some future benefit. Whenever they arise in consciousness, that is fine. When they don't, so be it. They may be remembered or they may be forgotten, and come up whenever they do. These affirmations – at their heart – are not addressing the individual in any capacity, so it really doesn't matter.

*What can this affirmation give me? What can it do for me?* The answer is found to be 'nothing'. And then the ego gradually loosens its grip. For, what use does the ego have of something from which it cannot derive its sense of self from, or cannot add to itself?

For some seekers, reading them just once would be enough and then the affirmations would naturally arise whenever they are supposed to. For others with a more disciplined approach, they could write them down and place them by their bedside to read every night. It really does not matter as long as it is done according to one's natural inclination. Slowly but surely, they would sink in deeper and deeper. Maharaj would often say: 'My concepts, if implanted in you, will destroy all other words and concepts.'

This statement of Maharaj is the real joker in the pack, the mother of all Trojan horses if you will. The very fact that you heard or read the affirmation meant that it has already been accepted by your awareness, as it arose in it. To put it more accurately, it has appeared within awareness and, therefore, that itself is the acceptance of it. Therefore, if 'you' choose to reject the affirmation and laugh it off, it is already too late as the seed has already been planted. Besides, awareness does not reject anything. What would the awareness of existence reject? The rejection is by a separate 'me' with its judgements and dislikes. But, as far as Maharaj was concerned, the game was already over. The battle was won before it was even fought!

I was pleasantly surprised (and found it to be a validation of what I felt, even though it was not required) to read much later on that Maharaj said: 'You don't

MAHARAJ AND THE TROJAN HORSE OF CONSCIOUS PRESENCE

need to worry. My teachings are already planted in your heart. They will sprout in due course. Simply have faith. There is no need to worry.'[2]

However, it must be noted that by saying that the affirmation will arise whenever it is supposed to, it does not mean it will arise only as a string of words – spoken or unspoken. That might happen initially, but soon it is found that it arises as the Understanding, and such arising can take place spontaneously or in response to a particular situation. Over time one will stabilise in that as the ground of one's being, instead of the habitually conditioned reaction of the ego to various situations it encounters in daily living.

Another point that must be noted is that failure in this approach is impossible. At a mundane level, if one was affirming for a dream home, relationship, and so on, one might not get what one desired even though one had been sincere in one's practice. This could lead to tremendous frustration at the failure to manifest one's desire through the process of affirmations. On the flip side, you may have the desire fulfilled for whatever it is that you have affirmed, but that very object could turn out to be something which makes you feel miserable later.

With Maharaj's affirmations there is nothing you are adding to yourself, be it in terms of material objects, relationships with others, and so on. Rather, it is a process of stripping away; of subtraction, so that the 'real you' shines forth in all its glory. It reminds me of Antoine de Saint-Exupéry's famous quote, 'Perfection is not when nothing more can be added, but when nothing more can be taken away.'

What's more, the affirmation reiterates what one already is; not what one wants to become but affirms it in the present tense in order to make it manifest. For example, if one wants to be in a loving relationship with a partner, some new age teachings would suggest an affirmation like: 'I am in a loving relationship at this moment.' With the power of the affirmation and visualisation, the result would supposedly manifest if practiced in the prescribed method.

With Maharaj's affirmations, it is like taking an exam in which you simply cannot fail. As mentioned earlier, the dictionary definition of 'affirmation' is 'a declaration of the truth or existence of something'. What could be closer to this than 'I am'?

The meaning of the *Mahavakyas* – the great sentences of Advaita Vedanta – is meant to be realised through direct experience. As far as Maharaj was concerned, it was already everyone's direct experience that they 'are'. His teachings were completely aligned with the scriptures even though he suggested not reading the scriptures at an intellectual level in order to garner theoretical knowledge, but rather to enquire into the nature of one's own 'beingness' for true knowledge to dawn.

It is clearly noticed that for some of the affirmations and reflections given below, Maharaj suggested that they be said preferably before sleeping. This is because at the end of the day, when the thinking mind recedes into the background as one enters the 'sleeping zone', a lesser resistance is put up by the separate 'me' to the statement being affirmed. These affirmations and reflections would, in fact, even help the thinking mind to quieten down, thus enabling a good night's sleep.

Other affirmations are to be done in the waking state. Again, 'done' is not really the apt word for they naturally arise whenever they are supposed to, bringing much peace and lightness to a situation, moreso to a stressful one. Whatever is 'done' is done by the separate 'me' and none of these affirmations can be 'done' as such, as they don't involve the 'me' but point back to the 'I am', the conscious presence in which everything that goes on in our lives arises and into which everything dissolves.

What a relief this approach is. You simply cannot fail, and this point cannot be reiterated enough.

Talking of failure reminds me of a conversation I had a few years ago with a doctor from Australia. He mentioned how one of his patients, who was at an advanced stage of cancer, enrolled for a course in 'attracting abundance and positivity in one's life'. He had been interviewed prior to enrolling and the assessment was that the course would have a positive effect on his health. He was quite convinced with the presentation made by the course facilitators, especially when he was told that he could be on his way to recovery if he followed the practice. However, even though he was diligent with all the practices that were prescribed, his condition only kept getting worse. As he was nearing the end of his days, he asked the course facilitators why things hadn't worked out as he hadn't improved. To this they replied that he was not visualising and affirming good health with *all* his heart.

Hearing this, I said, 'If someone facing death did not affirm good health with all his heart, I don't know who would!' The doctor nodded in agreement saying that was exactly his response. This lad passed away with a load of guilt for not wishing 'from his heart' to get better. He would have died a more peaceful death as a natural result of his illness, instead of with the stigma of being a failure slapped on him during his last days, and burdened with the guilt of not having been sincere enough to save himself.

Maharaj's affirmations point directly to the heart of existence. They are not addressed to the mind – the 'thinking mind' of the ego. There is no question of not putting one's heart into them.

Here are Maharaj's affirmations in all their pristine purity. They have a sutra-like quality and take the form of simple statements or reflections. Before the statement, or after it, comes a sentence or two as spoken by Maharaj, which I have included so that they are read in the context of what he was suggesting.

*'I am luminous, I am like ether, I am formless, pure and bodiless.'*

This should be your intense and speechless meditation every day – before going to sleep at least. And in course of time you will certainly attain to the state. This is what your Guru says: do not forget it.[3]

*'I am without a body and everything is perceived through my own light.'* This must be firmly established within.[4]

Make the mind i.e. prana say, *'My true nature is indestructible and eternal.'*

The mind will disappear; there will be the manifest Brahman Itself (thoughts disappear and pure Consciousness shines).[5]

Without pronouncing words, say, *'I am formless, desireless and pure as space. My sense 'I am' is of the nature of God.'*[6]

*'Many impure thoughts have come and gone away, but I am immutable, I am infinite, I am the Truth.'*
Sleep with these thoughts and all those impure thoughts are absolved.[7]

*'It is only because I am, that I see the world and think of God; therefore God is because I am. If I am not, God is not.'*
I will give you a formula which will do everything for you: Think continuously in terms of 'I am God; there is no God without me.' When you are firmly established in this, whatever is unimportant will gradually fall away.

A step further: I have told you to say 'I am God', but now what I am getting at is not just the words 'I am God' but that which was prior to the understanding of the words. That is God and that is you, not the words.

The postman comes here to deliver the mail. He may be a small man but he is fully aware that he represents the government. My feeling that I am, is the registration of the presence of God.[8]

Let me gladden your hearts by giving you a couple of tips. In spite of whatever I say, I know you will continue on your 'self-improvement' course and keep looking for tips...

1. Make it a habit to think and speak in the passive tense. Instead of 'I see something' or 'I hear something', why not think in the passive way: 'Something is seen' or 'Something is heard'? The perception will then not be on the basis of an action by the phenomenal entity but on the basis of an event or occurrence. In due course, the pseudo-entity 'I' will recede into the background.

2. Before going to sleep at night, spend about 10 minutes sitting relaxed both in body and mind, taking your stand that 'you' are not the body-mind construct but the animating consciousness, so this idea will impregnate your being throughout the period of your sleep.[9]

I'll tell you only one thing... Go on humming 'I am' without words, the unstruck sound.[10]

End Notes:

1 The Trojan Horse was the deception that the Greeks employed to enter the city of Troy and gain victory over the Trojans after a fruitless ten-year siege. The Greeks constructed a huge wooden horse in which they hid a select force of warriors inside and left the 'gift' of the wooden horse outside the city gates. While the Greeks pretended to sail away, the Trojans pulled the horse into their walled city as a victory trophy. That night the Greek force crept out of the horse and opened the gates for the rest of the Greek army which had sailed back under the cover of night. The Greeks entered and destroyed the city of Troy, thus decisively ending the war.

   Metaphorically speaking, a 'Trojan Horse' has come to mean any trick or deception employed that causes a target to invite an enemy into a securely protected bastion.

2 *The Last Days of Nisargadatta Maharaj* – S. K. Mullarpattan, Yogi Impressions Books Pvt. Ltd., Mumbai, 2006.

3 *Self-knowledge and Self Realisation* – Nisargadatta Maharaj, Shree Nisargadatta Ashram, Khetwadi, Bombay, 1963.

4 *Meditations with Sri Nisargadatta Maharaj*, Yogi Impressions Books Pvt. Ltd., Mumbai, 2014, p. 47.

5 *Ibid.*, p. 115.

6 *Ibid.*, p. 142.

7 *Seeds of Consciousness* – Nisargadatta Maharaj, Chetana Pvt. Ltd., 1997.

8 *Seeds of Consciousness* – Nisargadatta Maharaj, Chetana Pvt. Ltd., 1997.

9 *Pointers from Nisargadatta Maharaj*, Chetana Pvt. Ltd., 1996.

10 *Seeds of Consciousness* – Nisargadatta Maharaj, Chetana Pvt. Ltd., 1997.

# PATTERNS: THE CRY OF THE EGO

Most people are always on a quest to improve themselves. This quest is either to develop positive traits in our personality, or to remove negative traits. We wish to acquire qualities we do not have, as we perceive that lack of qualities as negative. Or, we wish to remove certain qualities that we do have, as we perceive those qualities to be negative. Either way, we view ourselves in a 'negative' sense, so to speak. With this in mind, some make the effort and read books on self-help, others visit spiritual teachers or counsellors, yet others go to temples, mosques, churches, and so on. More often than not, we are embroiled in trying to get rid of the perceived 'negative' that is an aspect of who we already are.

However, the point is that while we may feel that we have identified core issues in our personality that need to be ironed out and work towards addressing them, that's just the tip of the iceberg. The bulk of these personality traits are unconscious – we don't even know they exist. They have crept up on us without our conscious knowledge. So, if we feel we have achieved results on our path of self-improvement, we need only remember the fact that there is a smorgasbord of 'unpleasant' personality traits yet to be identified by us.

With regard to these traits, more often than not it takes another to point them out to us. It could be a family member, friend, co-worker or even a stranger. And, more often than not, we find ourselves denying that these traits exist. Denial is the first line of defence of the ego. Of course we will deny it, for we are not consciously aware of it in the first place. And sometimes we deny it even when we are conscious.

In my interactions with people over the years, I came across some interesting patterns being played out in which the unconscious activity engaged in by the mischievous ego surfaced. Seeing this opened my mind to how covert the operations of the ego are. Whenever I saw this occurring in other people, it made me wonder how deep some traits were embedded in my own psyche. It is obviously easier to spot these in others than in oneself.

While reading about these incidents, you may feel a sense of familiarity with either one or another pattern, as you may be aware of harbouring a similar trait in yourself or you may remember having observed that pattern in others. However, as mentioned earlier, the latter is more likely to be the case as one is rarely conscious of what all is deeply embedded in one's own personality.

### The stifled voice of the ego

One day a lady who owned a yoga studio visited my office to explore the possibility of showcasing and selling some of the books that we publish. She was soft-spoken and of a gentle disposition. After exchanging a few pleasantries she remarked that she found the hustle-bustle and noise of office environments quite disturbing and so requested if I could close the glass door of my cabin. I mostly keep the door open unless there is a confidential meeting in progress, which is rare. I had visited enough offices to know that ours is perhaps one of the quieter ones. Nevertheless, I readily agreed and got up to close the door. Once I settled back into my chair, I was taken aback at what happened next. The level of her voice, which had so far been soft and gentle, suddenly rose to a higher pitch. She started talking rather loudly even though we were having a normal conversation... so much so, that I wondered if the staff members were getting disturbed by her rather loud voice. When she laughed at something I said, it was at an even higher pitch and I noticed a couple of my colleagues peeking into my cabin through the glass, to see what the noise was all about.

At first I was quite perplexed at this dramatic change in her manner of speaking for, if at all, her voice should have become even softer once the cabin door had been closed. What had most likely caused this change in her then became clearer. Perhaps she wanted to be heard, and the very thought of 'office noise' made her feel that her voice would be drowned out and, consequently, she would not have the full attention of the person she was speaking to.

This pattern was perhaps playing itself out again and again during her interactions with people in different situations. A pattern which is repetitive tends to be need-based.

When could this pattern have set in? It was most likely to have occurred in her childhood when she felt the need to be heard else her views would be drowned out. For example, a possible scenario could be that she needed to make herself heard to her father, especially if she had siblings. A particular scene from childhood perhaps was being repeatedly played out (unconsciously, of course) as she grew older. This developed into a 'pattern' in which she would speak at a louder pitch even when it was unwarranted. Why? In order for the need of the ego to feel, 'I am important', 'I am in control here', 'I want to be heard'. For it is in the nature of the ego to seek attention, to feel it is in charge of a situation. With the passing years, any authoritative figure could take on the role of someone she looked up to, and this could result in the pattern getting triggered.

In the present situation, I perhaps played the role of someone she looked up to. Therefore there was the cry of the ego to be heard.

If this pattern was not in her field of awareness it would keep on repeating itself, and if and when it was brought to her attention, a possible response would be one of denial. What's more, the pattern is the comfort zone of the ego that has by now been conditioned to behave in a certain manner; something it is familiar with. The ego does not want to get rid of the pattern. However, if she did accept it when it was brought to her notice, then comes the arduous task of trying to break the pattern.

Arduous, because the individual ego is consciously trying to break a pattern that it did not consciously create in the first place.

Arduous, because for the pattern to break the 'need' has to be identified, and one doesn't know how early in the individual's lifetime the need originated.

Arduous, because the individual views the pattern as something that is being done by 'me', which 'I' should not be doing.

And finally, arduous because no matter how much the 'me' tries to break the pattern, awareness of the pattern generally comes only after the pattern has repeated itself.

The main problem is that the ego claims the pattern as 'my' pattern. It is this view that needs to be corrected by viewing it objectively: not as 'my' pattern, but as 'a' pattern. It must be clearly seen that it is a pattern that has developed due to life circumstances and situations one has faced, especially in the formative years. In other words, it is a consequence of one's conditioning at home (parental inputs and the sibling factor), school and college, as well as the socio-economic, religious and cultural environments that one grew up in and was influenced by. Over none of these did one have any direct control.

**Awareness of a pattern**

Once the pattern is brought into one's awareness and gets acknowledged to exist, then there can be an acceptance of the pattern. When it arises next it might yet go unrecognised and the awareness may come later that it had arisen. By all means, one could try to be aware of the pattern when one repeats it or, even better, before it arises. But one should not berate oneself at the failure to stop the pattern. That would only aggravate the situation because berating oneself every time the pattern arises would be the creation of yet another pattern! The ego is really good at creating patterns since they serve its need.

The crucial point is that whenever a pattern is recognised, it is recognised in awareness. Whether it is recognised before the onset of the pattern, during the pattern playing itself out or after it has been played out – the recognition takes place in awareness. The recognition of the pattern takes place by that which is not identified with the pattern. No wonder the ego – the 'me' – gets so frustrated in its attempts to see and then break the pattern. It is so difficult to see the pattern simply because the pattern is a consequence of the ego – it's like trying to see the hair on one's head.

A deliberate attempt to catch a pattern through vigilance of the 'me' will, in fact, take one further away from the awareness that is the ground on which the recognition of the pattern takes place. The only way to see it is with the mirror of awareness and it is not the ego that holds up the mirror of awareness, even if it thinks it does. Awareness is that in which the ego and its antics are reflected; it is in awareness that the witnessing of the pattern takes place.

## Awareness is not a function of the ego

The ego, that is the thinking mind, cannot witness the pattern. The ego observes the pattern as an individual, and judges it as good or bad. Awareness is not an act of the ego. Awareness does not judge a pattern. Awareness is awareness of the pattern, witnessed in an impersonal light. When it arises next and is witnessed, it is then seen that the pattern is not one's enemy; it is seen in a more compassionate light, thanks to the light of awareness that shines on it. Why is it seen that the pattern is not one's enemy? Simply because it is not the ego witnessing the pattern, therefore it is no longer 'my' pattern. Awareness does not have enemies; awareness takes no prisoners. Nothing is judged as 'bad' in awareness for awareness is the absence of the one who judges – the separate 'me'. For that matter, nothing is judged as 'good' either!

It must be clearly understood that you cannot try to be aware of the pattern, for the simple reason that awareness is the absence of the 'you' that is trying to be aware of it. By trying to 'be aware' of the pattern, the ego is trying to take ownership of the awareness; a case of the arsonist taking charge of the fire engines!

The ego thinks that if it is in a constant state of awareness and vigilance, it will then be able to prevent the pattern from repeating. It has laid an elaborate trap to catch the wild elephant called 'pattern'. This is like digging an elephant pit right where you are standing. The ego itself keeps falling into the pit in its efforts to break the pattern, while the pattern keeps roaming the ranges of our life freely, trampling all over our peace. For the individual to try being in a state of constant awareness is to take yet another step away from awareness, making one go round and round chasing awareness like a dog chasing its own tail.

Half the battle is won when one views a pattern no longer as 'my' pattern but witnesses it as 'a' pattern. The other half is won when one is no longer involved psychologically in the pattern after it arises; brooding all the time that one's efforts to prevent it have been in vain. With this approach, over time, or sometimes suddenly, a possible outcome could be that the pattern stops repeating itself as it starts burning in the fires of awareness.

All that can be truly brought to the pattern is awareness. And 'you' can't bring the pattern to 'your' awareness every time it is repeated. Who does it then? It is God. The Source. Consciousness. The same Force that created the pattern in the first place; the same Force that brought the pattern to our awareness and made us recognise it as a pattern. One needs to trust the Force to take us further and not leave us stranded.

Whether a pattern is broken or not is ultimately God's will. And if it does break, whether it takes a few years to break or it's immediate, is also God's will. With God playing such a big role in all of this, why not trust God to resolve the whole issue of the pattern by just stepping aside and letting Him do His job?

### The noise about silence

Sometime back I met a friend – a woman with a very pleasing personality, over a cup of coffee. She used to attend the talks of my spiritual teacher whenever she was in Mumbai. Long after the teacher passed away, she called to say she was in town and so we met up. For over 30 minutes, she talked in a continuous monologue on how much she loved 'silence'!

The stories kept pouring forth: 'I loved the silence when I was walking in the forests in Scotland… I love the silence when I am sipping my cup of tea sitting on the balcony and looking out towards the horizon… I love the silence when I am taking my morning walk… I love the silence of the late night hours… I love the silence, I love the silence, I love the silence!'

I then recalled that whenever we met up after the talks we attended, the subject of silence and stillness would inevitably come up as a topic of discussion.

What might have happened in this case? Perhaps it was the concept of silence that she loved. It was something deep down she wished to experience. She was perhaps not at peace with herself; there were too many thoughts racing through the mind.

True silence, the inner stillness, would not have the need to express itself for almost an hour and in so many words. When you are truly silent, 'you' are not there; silence is. Later on, the 'you' takes ownership of the silence and claims that it likes it, just like it takes ownership of everything else.

Now, if she experienced another person as being silent or just deeply appreciating silence, then that person would become someone she would want to be like. In this case, I guess it was me. I was the quiet type so it was a relatively easy conclusion to draw. Why did she want to be like me?

Because she likes that attribute and feels she does not have it herself. This pattern (of constantly talking about the love for silence) would keep playing out, as it was need-based. What's more, it is being played out in unawareness as she is not aware that she is not silent, although she thinks that she is. Looking back at that meeting, I thought it was actually quite a sweet thing to witness, for the cry of the ego was expressed with such innocence even though it took so many words to do it. It was a cry of wanting to be in silence; wanting to be the absence of the noise that typifies the thinking mind of the ego. You can only crave for that which you already know, else why would you crave it?

One knows that true silence has been experienced in the peace of deep sleep. And yet that experience is not the experience of some 'one', as deep sleep is the absence of the ego, the one that takes ownership of an experience. No 'one' experiences deep sleep. It has also tasted that silence in the waking state, when the mind is quiet and not engaged in incessant thinking, or when there is a gap between two thoughts. So even though the entire monologue was at a conceptual level, deep down there was a recognition of that which is its true nature.

**The unconscious business of patterns**

One day, a close friend of mine told me about his friend whom he used to meet quite often but had now stopped meeting. The reason they stopped meeting was that whenever they would get together, the friend along with his wife, would talk of nothing else except the couple's flourishing business. They would go on and on about how well their export business was doing. They were so consumed by their story that they would never enquire about how his business was faring. My friend said that matters reached a point where, during the last time they met, he told both of them off saying they were too consumed with themselves to bother about the well-being of others. The couple felt bad, said they were sorry, and then immediately enquired about his business. But it had come too late... the bridges had already been burnt and they drifted apart.

While I heard him out, I once again was surprised about the lack of awareness; not that of the couple, but his own. For all the years we had known each other, he never asked me how my business was going but when I would enquire about his, he would go on and on endlessly.

What had happened in this case? Generally, this happens when one wants to be like someone whom one looks up to, and therefore unconsciously imitates. Perhaps he wanted to be like his friend whom he looked up to as a role model and therefore imitated. He wanted to be as successful and wanted to do as well in his business but felt there was some inadequacy, whether in the business or in his personality. In all likelihood, he was immersed in thinking about himself and was actually playing the role of the friend with me; once again in total unawareness. It's not that it was done intentionally.

We should be careful while criticising people for it might just be that we are being criticised by others for the same reason, keeping us mired in the dualism of life as we know it and getting stuck in a vortex of judgements that go round and round in circles – like the Ouroboros swallowing its own tail. In judgement, we act as if we are the subject and the other the object, without realising that we are the object in the other's eyes. Thus, we play God – the Original Subject – and thereby commit what spiritual teacher Ramesh Balsekar would refer to as 'the original sin'. Little do we realise that we all are played by God, the ultimate non-judgemental Judge, the One who does not judge because God is 'what is', the totality of manifestation, and not a perspective from a speck somewhere in a tiny corner of the universe, separate from the rest of it.

## Being comfortable with oneself

There is a young lad of 28, whom I know. He does not have the disposition to work and is quite comfortable with it, as he realises this is his nature. So how does he spend his days? He says that his true calling is to 'give of himself to others'. For example, if he makes new friends, he will spend hours with them when they are at home. He will also do things for them like take the dog for a walk, do their grocery shopping, hang out with their parents and take them out for movies, shopping, visits to doctors, and so on.

This all sounds very nice and appears to be a genuine case of living for others. For he could be altruistically motivated, and his nature is not suited to work in order to earn a living. On the other hand, could it be possible that this is a covert attempt by the ego to justify its existence to itself, proving that it is doing something in life that is worthwhile? After all, it was a pattern that made him spend endless hours with others, being of some kind of service to them. If we were to view it in this light, then the possibility emerges that doing all this was proof to himself that he was doing something worthwhile in his life. In other words, the pattern is propelled by his own need to prove to himself that he is productive, and it is not the need of the people he is with. In doing so, he feels valued and his existence gets meaning.

If behaviour is not need-based, then one is fine doing one's own thing, which is not determined by other people. You could spend long hours by yourself going for a walk, watching the sun go down, sitting at home sipping coffee while reading a book, and so on. Of course, you would be there to help others or 'offer your time', but in such a case it would not be a pattern, for there is no 'need' that needs to be satisfied.

The ego could trick one into believing that one is being 'of value' to others but deep down does it really feel that way, or is it trying to fulfil a lack, or a vacuum? Once again, this is an unconscious pattern and could even go unresolved as there may be no one to bring it to the notice of the individual. This would more likely be the case simply because it seems such a noble endeavour. If so, it would be his destiny to play this pattern out over the years. If the pattern was to come to his awareness, and the need identified, that would be part of the destiny as well. The whole point is: 'Was he at peace, or did he think he was, or did he wish he was?'

All in all, living for others does not come naturally to everyone. And, enhancing people's lives by giving of one's time is truly genuine giving. Whether deep down he *feels* – and not *thinks* – he is at peace, only he would know.

The ego can perform somersaults to make itself believe it has peace of mind. You are truly comfortable with others only when you're comfortable with yourself. However, the ability to spend long hours with others is not an indication that you're comfortable with others and with yourself, if it is occurring as a pattern to fulfil a need. One who can live in solitude has a deep understanding of life. He is alone, but never lonely. He is whole, he is complete, and he is happy to be in his own company. And, more often than not, he finds that more and more people want to spend time with him, rather than the other way around.

In conclusion, patterns give us the following insights when seen in the light of Understanding:

1. Just as someone else has patterns that he or she is not aware of, so do I. This is a humbling thought. The more you see these patterns in others, the more it makes you wonder how many are stuffed into your own Pandora's Box. Humility is a strange thing. Ramesh Balsekar used to say: 'True humility is never recognised as such by the one who has it.' I recently read an interview a UK-based reporter conducted with one of Bollywood's leading male stars. She came down heavily on him, and the Indian press in turn came down heavily on her in support of the star. What she had pointed out was that all through the interview, this star went on and on about how humble he was!

2. In many cases, what we see in others is something that we have seen, felt or experienced in ourselves at some point of time or another. For example, if we say that someone is full of jealousy and envy for people who have done better in life, it means that we know what it is to be jealous and therefore have judged him of that. Therefore, judging others based on their patterns is in fact judging oneself. And, at the end of the day, it's meaningless.

3. Who reacts to another's pattern? It is 'my ego' that reacts to a pattern. So, if I find myself reacting, I can rest assured that it is an egoic reaction. For example, if I find myself gossiping and maligning someone because of his or her pattern, it is then a reaction rooted in unawareness. Conscious Presence accepts people for what they are. This does not mean one needs to suffer another's company if one doesn't want to. All it means is that one doesn't judge the 'other' because of their pattern.

4. When patterns in others are recognised without a knee-jerk reaction in us, it is a sign that the understanding is quite deep. This means we are rooted in awareness. Or rather, awareness is rooted in us.

5. It is witnessed that people are not their patterns. Their patterns are a result of their conditioning and genes. Who they are in essence is who I am – it is the same Consciousness functioning through us, which provides us with the awareness that we exist.

6. All patterns belong to the world of the ego, which in the peace of deep sleep thankfully disappears. In deep sleep there are no patterns, for 'you' do not exist. What a relief – no patterns to worry about in deep sleep! And That which is pattern-less prevails in the waking state too, else how would one know one slept well? Consciousness is the bedrock of our being, whether as impersonal consciousness in the deep sleep state, or as identified consciousness in the waking or dreaming state. So, even when we are playing out our patterns in the waking state, the ground on which it is being played out is 'Peace'.

With this understanding comes a tremendous ease in one's relationship with others whether they be family members, close friends or even strangers. More importantly, one is completely at ease in one's relationship with oneself. This results in being comfortable with oneself, as well as being comfortable with others. What better pattern could one hope for?

---

A note by integral psychotherapist Dr. Sonera Jhaveri is provided in the Appendix.

# SONG OF THE UNBORN

Deep sleep is my natural state. It never leaves me, even in the waking state. It never leaves me – no matter how convinced I am that I am not in deep sleep when I am awake. Could one ask for a more loyal friend?

Where could what I am in deep sleep go when I am awake? If it did go away then how could I say, 'I slept well'? Something needs to be present in *both* the deep sleep state as well as the waking state for me to say, 'I slept well'. *Something* needs to *know* that 'I slept well'. 'Who slept well?' is the question that begs an answer. The one who is making the statement in the waking state is the one who is not present during deep sleep, for in deep sleep one does not know that one exists. Yet, the one making the statement says, 'I slept well'! That which is actually present in deep sleep does not make the statement in the waking state. The question of making the statement does not arise, for it would mean there is 'someone' present in the deep sleep state to make the statement in the waking state, whereas it is the very absence of 'someone' that is the presence of the peace of deep sleep.

Yet one says, 'I slept well'. What a Divine irony!

That which is present in deep sleep is the Presence

that is ever present, without which 'you' would be a dead body. In the waking state, the absence of the individual 'me and my story' and all its rumblings, is the palpable presence of that very Presence. Sometimes, we feel this palpable presence in the company of sages. We feel calm in their presence. It is the absence of the sense of separation, and all doership associated with it, that is the hallmark of their waking state through which the Presence shines. For the rest of us, deep sleep proves that the Presence is ever present despite the interference of 'me and my story'.

Therefore, you can never *not* be the presence of Presence, for you can never *not* be what you are in deep sleep. What a relief that thought is!

Presence is the ever fresh canvas of our inner sky. The sometimes light, sometimes ominous clouds of 'me and my story' are always passing across it. When you look up, most of the time clouds are floating around here and there, obscuring the clear blue sky. In the same way, an accumulation of conditioning, memories and events that together form a vapour-like mist of a 'me' floats around here and there, obscuring the view of the true You.

Of course, you cannot *not* be what you are in the waking state – a separate 'me' that is an accumulation of various events that have happened to that 'me' and through that 'me' in the waking state, endowing 'me' with all the conditioning that I have received right from the moment I was born. It is on this basis that I perform my so-called actions. Yet again, and more importantly, you cannot *not* be That which you are in the deep sleep state – the *absence* of the separate 'me' that dissolves in deep sleep.

Laugh out loud; cry your heart out, as you go through the rough and tumble of daily living. And know that while you are building monuments of your pains and pleasures, That which prevails in deep sleep prevails all along. It is the bedrock of your very being for without it, 'you' cannot *be*. It is the foundation upon which you apparently build the ice palaces of your joys and sorrows in the waking state, and all that goes to make for the ups and downs in your life. 'Apparent' because 'you' melt away in the peace of deep sleep. 'You' the architect assigned the task of building all the ice palaces in the waking state, are made to perform a magician's disappearing act as you melt away in deep sleep – only to re-emerge as a barrage of impressions bursting forth from beneath the surface of the ice, projecting all the images that make up the next day of your life.

All that you go through in the waking state is nothing but a song to the unsung hero – the peace of deep sleep. Born in movement, the waking 'you' runs around the theatre of your life unknowingly paying homage to That which is unmoved and still. Yet, however much the shenanigans of daily living hassle us, we are usually at peace for one-third of our lives, for one-third of our lives are spent in deep sleep. And, whenever we say, 'I didn't sleep well' it just means that the villain of the piece, 'me and my story', remained on the stage. The roller-coaster of 'me and my story' kept us awake when we should have been asleep. The presence of 'me', when I am supposed to be asleep, is the absence of the peace of deep sleep. For deep sleep is the absence of the presence of 'me'!

Every day a great migration takes place: when we go to bed and when we wake up. *Who goes to sleep? Who wakes up? Who's asking the question? Who wants to know the answer? Who cares?* Certainly not That which is present in deep sleep. In the waking state, ego identification takes over – the same identification that then says, 'I slept well'. This is the one who cares. Yet, it is still an aspect of the same Consciousness that prevails in deep sleep. Consciousness is all there is, whether 'impersonal' in the deep sleep state or 'identified' as the 'me' in the waking and dreaming states. 'Impersonal' and 'identified' are aspects of the one Consciousness that is the continuum that prevails through the deep sleep and waking states, and a pilgrimage from one to the other takes place every day.

You cannot *not* be that which you already are: the presence of the peace of deep sleep. Therefore, where is the question of attaining peace, when you are already That? How can one acquire what one already has, what one already is? How can the 'you' in the waking state ever achieve the peace of the deep sleep state, when the peace of the deep sleep state is the absence of the 'you' that is present in the waking state? The one who says, 'I want to be at peace' is the same one who says, 'I slept well'.

How united we are in deep sleep: no arguments, conflicts, wars, blame, condemnation, guilt, shame, separation, 'us', 'them' and so on and so forth, *ad nauseum*. We have no problems in deep sleep; the trouble begins when we wake up and identification with 'me and my story' takes over – identification with caste, creed, race, religion, etc.

When will the profound peace of deep sleep prevail in the waking state? The only answer is yet another question: Who wants to know? The ego, which disappears in deep sleep, wants to know how it can be That which is its very absence. The cloud wants to know what the clear blue sky looks like!

The fact is that the presence of the peace of deep sleep does prevail in the waking state, when our thinking mind is not running rampant like a herd of wild elephants. It is present when we are simply witnessing without judging. Then the peace of 'what is' shines through. It is the peace of 'I am' – the impersonal awareness of being, without the separate 'me' – 'I am Gautam', with its identification and doership, gate-crashing the party! It is the same 'I am' that prevails in deep sleep. The presence, the existence that prevails in deep sleep, becomes the impersonal awareness of being in the waking state (I am, I exist), which then gets extended into and clouded by 'I am Gautam'... and the show of 'me' operating in 'my' world begins once again.

Fortunately, sometimes an illuminating flash of lightning suddenly strikes. The statement, 'I slept well' is a window that offers a glimpse into this elusive peace. 'I slept well' is the ultimate proof that the peace of deep sleep can never leave us, even in the waking state.

The joker in the pack is that all this rationalising about deep sleep is taking place in the conscious waking state, while That which is prevalent in deep sleep has no need for or interest in such conceptualising. That which is, simply Is.

# REVERSING INTO THE FUTURE
## (THE FLOW OF LIFE)

What were you a 100 years before you were born?

Consciousness unaware of Itself – in other words, Potential Energy. And the nature of energy is 'potential' because it has to get activated sometime; else it would be dead matter.

Birth* is the activation of Potential Energy, which is the 'Big Bang' at the cosmic level. Consciousness-at-rest, unaware of Itself, has stirred. It has now become aware of Itself as 'I am'. 'I am.' 'I exist.'

Thus is Consciousness born as a child. The child, of course, does not say 'I am, I exist.' Rather 'amness' and 'existence' is there, which was not there prior to birth. It is the impersonal awareness of simply 'being'. Not being a personal 'I am this' or 'I am that' – but just 'I am'.

Therefore, Consciousness-at-rest has now become Consciousness-in-action.

The pure 'I am' is what is present in deep sleep. We exist, but in deep sleep we don't know that we exist. The 'impersonal consciousness' in deep sleep becomes 'identified consciousness' in the waking state. 'I am' becomes 'I am Gautam'.

This 'I am Gautam' is not the truth. For one, a truth is that which nobody can deny. If I were to visit another country

---

* Birth, in this instance, actually refers to the moment of conception.

and introduce myself to someone as 'I am Gautam', that person could well ask, 'How do I know that you are Gautam?' Another more relevant point is, how could 'I am Gautam' be the truth – be real – if it disappears in deep sleep? For it to be real, should it not remain present through both the deep sleep as well as the waking states?

So, if 'I am Gautam' does not continue through the deep sleep as well as waking states, then what does? The 'I am' does. Pure existence i.e. beingness, is the continuum through the deep sleep and waking states. It is that which allows one to say, 'I slept well' on waking up in the morning. The 'I am' is the only truth. No one can deny one's existence. To do so would, in fact, prove existence itself!

Death is the moment when Consciousness-in-action goes back to Consciousness-at-rest. Then Consciousness is no longer aware of Itself. We are now what we were a 100 years before we were born. Yet it must be emphasised that what we were a 100 years before we were born, is what we are now. They are not two, for the bedrock is Consciousness. Consciousness is all there truly is – whether as the Unmanifest Absolute, or the manifest, impersonal 'I am' of deep sleep and the personal 'I am Gautam' of the waking and dreaming states.

Similarly, the manifestation and the world as we know it is a reflection of the Source *within* Itself. In other words, it is a reflection within the Source – they are not two.

When we refer to the future, what future are we talking about if our future is ultimately going back to the same state before we were born? Are we really going into the future, or are we going back to the past? All we are doing is reversing into the future.

The big joke about the future is that from the moment of birth, our so-called future starts diminishing up till the moment of death. So the maximum stock of our 'future' is from the moment of our birth. What a short-lived future that is, as compared to the future that goes on after the moment of death for hundreds of years! Of course, Consciousness-at-rest – unaware of Itself – has no concept of time, which is but an aberration that comes into being from the moment of birth when Consciousness becomes aware of Itself – 'I am'.

As Nisargadatta Maharaj would say: 'What were 'you' a 100 years before you were born?' The same would you be a 100 years after 'you' died.

So, is it really worth worrying about the phenomenal future when one knows that one's ultimate destiny is the death of the ego, and the death of all conceptual problems? Your destiny is 'Peace' – a 'peace that passeth understanding', for there is no 'one' to understand anything after death.

Isn't it true that we die to our problems every night when the peace of deep sleep descends upon us? For a third of our life, we have no problems – the problems are not real because they do not exist. Yet they seem so real in the waking state – just as dreams appear to be real in the dream state. Our problems are not real because all problems belong to the 'me' – which itself is not real. How could it be real if it disappears in the peace of deep sleep? The peace of deep sleep also prevails in the waking state, for that which is present in deep sleep is also present in the waking state, which allows us to say that 'I slept well'.

We are so afraid of death, which is nothing but a prolonged deep sleep from which there is no waking up. Has anyone been afraid of deep sleep?

Are we truly living in the present moment – the 'Now' – if...

*'The present moment – here and now – is basically in a different dimension from the 'present' in the flow of time from the past to the future, or from the future to the past. In the flow of time, there is actually no 'present' because perception of any event, its registration in the brain, needs a certain time – the tenth of a second – after the actual happening of the event. This means that, in actuality, we are always living in the past. The here-and-now witnessing the flow of time is like a spectator watching the flow of the river – not from within the river but from the bank or from the top of a culvert across the river.'*

– Ramesh Balsekar

We are hurtling through life just like a river hurtles towards the ocean to meet its ultimate destiny – that of merging with the ocean. No matter what obstacles the river faces, it meanders and finds its way around them to reach the ocean. The river does not perceive the obstacles as obstacles, but merely embraces 'what is' as it wraps itself around rocks and boulders in its path.

It is the 'thinking mind' of the ego that labels obstacles as obstacles to be avoided or surmounted with every effort possible – in order to reach its goal. The goal of the ego is restricted in duration of time and, therefore, during the lifetime of the ego. As a result, the river of life gets polluted, toxic and murky with all the 'doing' to get somewhere, at some point in the future. What one loses sight of is the fact that 'some point in the future' still refers to the future as a river. When there is total acceptance of the inevitable merging of the river into the ocean, life is lived with fluid grace befitting the true nature of the river – water – meeting itself in the ocean.

One of my spiritual teacher's favourite jokes was: Mutt is struggling to drive the car up the hill. He has slammed the accelerator to the floor, but the climb is a steep one. Finally, the car reaches the top of the hill and Mutt heaves a sigh of relief. He turns to look at his co-passenger and says, 'Jeff, I am so glad we made it to the top. I did not tell you, but I feared that the car would roll back down as it was simply too steep a climb. It is quite possible that we would not have made it.'

'Oh no, Mutt, that would not have happened,' replied Jeff. 'You see, I had put the handbrake on.'

That is exactly how we are driving the car of our life on the road of daily living. The foot on the accelerator is the 'working mind' operating in the moment, to deal with the situation at hand. The handbrake is the 'thinking mind' of the ego, full of fears and insecurities of the future and regrets of the past, full of wanting things to be a specific way – 'what should be' and ignoring the here and now – 'what is'.

If only we could let go of our grip on incessant thinking, and let life flow like a river to the sea.

Many years ago, I read a book by C. W. Leadbeater in which he mentioned that he was deeply influenced by the content of a book called *The Stars and the Earth*. It had a great impact on me as well.

The gist of it was: When we see an object, we do so by means of rays of light that pass from the object that we see, to our eyes. The speed at which light travels is 186,000 miles per second, due to which we see an object in our environment almost instantly. However, things change when objects are at a great distance from us. For example, it takes over eight minutes for the light to travel to us from the sun. This means that when we are viewing the sun, we are actually viewing the 'past' of the sun. If the sun were to get extinguished, we would only come to know eight minutes after it did.

Now there are stars even further than the sun. It takes 50 years for light to travel from the Pole Star to us. So, if something were to happen to the Pole Star, we would happily have no clue of it during our incarnation on earth, and it would be witnessed by our children instead.

Then there are stars that are thousands of years away from us. That means, if something were to happen to a star that far away, we would only know of it after thousands of years.

This begets the question: Are we looking at the present, or at the past?

'The manifestation is a block,' as spiritual teacher Ramesh Balsekar would often say. He would also use the analogy of a ten-mile long painting where an individual is viewing the painting in the dark with the aid of a penlight, as he walks along it. He doesn't know what scenes will emerge as he walks along the painting, but the scenes are already there. Could it be that all future events are fixed, in a sense, and it is we who are moving towards them?

If indeed they are fixed, then wouldn't it mean that we are actually going back to our past? And, if we are going back into the past, doesn't it mean that while we consider ourselves moving into our future, we are actually reversing into it?

I am reminded of a narration I read of Ram Dass meeting Neem Karoli Baba. Ram Dass had an urge to meet his guru, while he was participating in a Vipassana course at Bodh Gaya. He left with a busload of 24 fellow seekers and when they reached the crossroads, the bus driver asked whether he should take the bus to Delhi, or on to Allahabad where the Kumbh Mela was being held. It was a tough decision as Ram Dass did not know where Maharaj-ji was.

He took a chance and pointed in the direction of Allahabad. This was around 10 am. Once they reached Allahabad, lo and behold, they saw Maharaj-ji walking by the side of the road. Maharaj-ji instructed them to follow him to someone's house and when they reached there, the woman of the house said he had given them a call asking her to prepare lunch for 25 people (24 plus the driver). Maharaj-ji had made the call to them at 6 am!

As Sir Oliver Lodge said in his address to the British Association at Cardiff: *'A luminous and helpful idea is that time is but a relative mode of regarding things; we progress through phenomena at a certain definite pace and this subjective advance we interpret in an objective manner, as if events moved necessarily in this order and at this precise rate. But that may be only one mode of regarding them. The events may be in some sense in existence always, both past and future, and it may be we who are arriving at them, not they which are happening. The analogy of a traveller in a railway train is useful; if he could never leave the train nor alter its pace he would probably consider the landscapes as necessarily successive and be unable to conceive their co-existence...'*\*

Usually, we think that A leads to B, B leads to C, and C leads to D, and so on. But the arrow of cause and effect is double-pointed. For D to happen – C had to happen, for C to happen – B had to happen, and so on. We are not really moving towards the future, but are simply reversing into it. An accident does not happen because we are at a particular place at a particular time. We 'had to be' at a particular place at a particular time because the accident 'had to happen'. The cause does not produce the effect. Because the effect had to happen, the cause had to be there. As the sage Vimalananda said: 'Cause is effect concealed, and effect is cause revealed.'

---

\* *Clairvoyance* – C. W. Leadbeater, The Theosophical Publishing House, Adyar, Madras, India.

If we can't see our future, it's as good as having our backs to it.

Think of a gust of wind blowing towards you. And you turn your back to it. You now feel the gust hitting your back. The wind moves past you, on your left and right, beyond your shoulders, arms and legs. If the wind had a colour – let's say blue – you would see streaks of blue emerging from behind you, going past your shoulders, hands and legs, into the past that is now actually ahead of you as you are looking at it.

The future, that has become the past, can be looked at. This is where we are at – the vantage point. And from this vantage point, we see that our vision has turned 180 degrees towards a new way of seeing – one that is no longer a cause-effect seeing: A leads to B leads to C leads to D, but rather seeing that for D to happen, C had to happen, for C to happen, B had to happen, and so on.

And what is the vantage point? It is the vantage point of the 'here and now' – the present moment. Actually, it's not even the moment as such for the moment becomes the past in no time, but pure Presence – conscious presence. That's what we are in our truest essence, without the taint of 'me and my story'.

What is the result of such seeing? Equanimity. Calm. A relaxed realisation that things are the way they were meant to be. A seeing that no longer constantly seeks a cause and effect relationship between events and happenings in one's life, and why things happened this way and not that way. A seeing that understands and accepts that for something to happen, a series of prior events had to happen over which in all likelihood we did not have any control.

This, of course, precludes the deeper understanding that 'Thy Will Be Done'. Whatever happens, happens because it is God's will. This understanding leads to a total acceptance of 'what is'. This in itself precludes an even deeper understanding – that we are not going forward into the future but rather going back into it. Back to where we came from… Home.

What does all this boil down to in our daily living?

It implies reversing into our true essence: the Consciousness that animates all beings.

This means not being mired in the dreary play of dualism of 'me' versus the 'other' but, rather, clearly seeing that there truly is no 'other' as all there is, is Consciousness. For it is in Consciousness that the 'other' appears. A seeing in which all judgements fall away, along with ill-will, spite, hatred, jealousy, blame, pride, arrogance, guilt and shame. Nobody truly 'does' anything as all there is, is the will of the Source i.e. Consciousness.

It means not taking ourselves to be the subject and the other as the object, and thereby pronouncing judgment upon the object, but realising that we too are objects in the other's eyes. In fact, we are all objects, with the same energy – Consciousness – functioning through all of us, just as electricity functions through different gadgets in the kitchen. Consciousness is the One True Subject.

It means not being buffeted between the banks of pleasure and pain; not to be constantly seeking only pleasure and not pain. There is an understanding that the flow of life is the duality of interconnected opposites – good and bad, beautiful and ugly, rich and poor, healthy children and handicapped children; accepting 'what is', whatever life brings, and accepting one's reaction to it. Not as 'my' reaction but 'a' reaction in a body-mind organism that appears to be mine.

Choosing pleasure over pain would be like the river trying its best to flow along only one of its banks, which is impossible!

And finally, in the words of Nisargadatta Maharaj:

'*You never want what's true. You want what you don't have and don't want what you already have, and so you suffer. It's so perplexing! Why not simply reverse it? Why not want what you have, and not want what you don't have? It's so simple! You can be happy; it's here for the taking. You want little things when you could have the entire universe and eternity.*'

With this understanding, life may not become easier but it will surely become simpler. This is what my spiritual teacher would say.

So simple, that we just don't get it.

---

Note: This essay is inspired by two phrases of Nisargadatta Maharaj that impacted me tremendously, and the understanding of which I received from my spiritual teacher Ramesh Balsekar who was Maharaj's disciple. The two phrases were:

1. He would ask seekers who visited him, 'What were you a 100 years before you were born?'

2. He would occasionally use the phrase, 'We are reversing into the future'.

# THE HERESY OF TRUE LOVE

*Will he continue liking me? Everything's going fine as of now, but how do I get him to continue liking me, once the initial attraction wears off? What should I do to ensure he does not leave me? Why does this fear or uncertainty keep hounding my relationship over and over again, with whichever man I meet?*

Sarah couldn't figure out why this pattern repeated itself in her relationship with men: the dread of losing the person after the initial excitement was over. This created enormous anxiety in her, which invariably jeopardised the relationship she was presently in. She sought answers from therapists as well as spiritual teachers, and would introspect for days on end, but could not find a satisfactory answer to her predicament.

One evening she was sitting alone having a cup of tea at an outdoor café. A rather unassuming man came up to her and asked if he could share her table, as all the other tables were taken. She nodded her assent and indicated the chair across from hers. She was pleased to note that he appeared to be a quiet type, as she really wasn't looking for company and wanted to spend a quiet evening by herself before heading home for the night.

They exchanged polite formalities and the usual comments about the weather. He asked if she was waiting for someone and hoped he wouldn't be intruding.

'No, it's quite alright… I am here by myself,' she said with a casual shrug of her shoulders.

'An attractive girl like you, and without a date for the evening?' he smiled. 'That's hard to believe! Perhaps destiny is giving you some breathing space until the right man comes along…'

'Ha! Tell me about it!' she said. 'No one is around long enough, they all drift away. Maybe it's something to do with me… probably I scare them away! I guess it has something to do with the baggage of fear that I lug around with me,' she said with an undertone of exasperation.

'Fear… Fear of what?' he queried.

One thing led to another as they began conversing about relationships and why they are seen to fail so often. She spoke about this pattern that kept repeating itself in her relations with men. She spoke frankly… after all, he was a total stranger. It felt more like talking her heart out to someone.

The man was a good listener – patient and attentive. His tea arrived. He dipped the teabag a couple of times and stirred it gently with a spoon. She had finished talking and then fell silent.

He let the silence continue for some moments. He took a few sips of his tea and then, putting the cup down, leaned forward and said, 'If you aren't in a hurry to leave, I would like to tell you a true story…'

'It's nicer sitting out here in the breeze than staring at the ceiling in the confines of my room,' she said, leaning back in her chair to hear what he had to say…

One day, the young prince of Egypt, Amenhotep, was crying his heart out to his mother: 'Why doesn't father love me, like he loves my brother? He doesn't pat my head or hug me like he used to earlier,' the child sobbed. 'What have I done wrong, Mummy?'

Her heart crumpled like a sheaf of papyrus and she felt crushed – she knew the reason why the father had turned away from his younger son. In fact, it was pretty much evident to everyone. Her husband, Pharaoh Amenhotep III, was no longer fond of his younger son as the boy was not turning out to be a strapping young lad like his older brother Thutmose who was athletic, well-built, and was already developing a commanding presence. His elder son made the Pharaoh proud whereas young Amenhotep was turning out to be a source of embarrassment. The lad was thin, weak and looked sickly. On top of that, the boy was not the least bit interested in athletics. Worse, the young lad appeared to be developing a mind of his own – always questioning everything.

'What have I done wrong, Mother?' the child cried his heart out. Queen Tiye fought hard to hold back her tears. She could not bear to see her younger son's plight. Cradling him in her arms, she consoled him: 'Shushhh, my child. Of course, your father loves you very much. Now go to sleep.'

Days and weeks went by. One evening, when young Amenhotep had not come back to the palace for his mid-day meal, the attendant complained to his mother, 'My Queen, what can I do? The young prince refuses to come indoors.

THE END OF SEPARATION

He seems to go into a trance every now and then. He just sits for hours, with his face turned towards the Aten.'

'Don't worry, I will go and bring him,' said the Queen on her way out to the gardens.

'Look Mummy, just look at the Aten,' exclaimed her son excitedly. 'See how bright and shining it is… lighting up everything under and around it! Aten makes no distinction between rich and poor, good and bad. It gives life to everything! I don't know why we worship our gods in dark chambers, they who grant us power and riches! Of what use is all that? Where would we all be without the Aten, Mummy? He is the one god we can see and, therefore, should worship. After all, the Aten showers his love equally on everything and everyone.'

The Queen was wonderstruck. 'How could one so young have such profound insight; where does this wisdom come from?' Other children his age were so busy playing around but Amenhotep was lost in another world, far removed from this one.

'Yes, my son, you are right,' she said agreeing with him. 'Come in now… it's time for your meal.' As they turned to go inside, the child stopped in his tracks and, tugging at his mother's gown, said, 'Mummy, if I was one day to rule the land like father, the only law I would have would be the 'Law of Love'… equal love towards everyone!'

The fond mother narrated this incident to her husband that night.

'Is that what he said?' shouted the Pharaoh. 'That son of yours has turned out to be worse than I imagined, not only in appearance but in his thoughts, deeds, and now… he utters words of heresy! I am thankful to the Goddess Isis for Thutmose; everyone will look up to him as Pharaoh once I am gone!'

Well, sometimes even pharaohs' writ is not engraved in stone and things don't always go according to their plans. Thutmose died young and, after the Pharaoh passed away, destiny crowned the sickly, young Amenhotep, Pharaoh of Egypt.

One day, without informing anyone, the young Pharaoh took off into the desert. His best friend waited impatiently for him. He was known to disappear every now and then and would at times be found in a trance, but he had never been so late before in returning home. When he finally came back late at night – he was a changed man. No one could quite put a finger on what it was that had changed about him.

After remaining silent for quite a long while, Amenhotep told his friend:

'Today, I have heard the voice of God; the voice of the Void; the voice that gave birth to the Aten – the first ray of the Absolute. I have heard the voice of 'The One and Only', that is both masculine and feminine, and the Source of all dualities.'

As he said this, his friend saw that Amenhotep's eyes blazed with fire; the fire of the sun. It appeared as if the Aten was shining through them... through almost every pore of his being.

Amenhotep then pronounced: 'From now on, I shall be known as 'Akhenaten'! I am the Beloved of Aten and I will dedicate myself to 'The One and Only God' for He is the embodiment of Love, Happiness and Peace.'

When his mother heard this pronouncement, her heart swelled with pride; she had always known he was no ordinary son even though everyone else, including his own father, had written him off. Yet, she felt a stab of pain go through her chest. She knew that the Egyptians were not yet ready to be ruled with a great love such as that of her son – a love so palpable and dazzlingly bright that it just might singe everything in its path.

As it turned out, Queen Tiye was proved right.

Akhenaten broke with tradition in several ways. He would walk up to his palace guards and say, 'Will you accept my friendship?' This was unheard of from a pharaoh and took them completely by surprise, and yet endeared him to them. On his visits to the city, he broke protocol by going around unaccompanied by guards. He and his wife Nefertiti would get off their chariot to mingle among the people. The people on the streets felt enveloped by the love, one that knew no boundaries, and flowed so naturally from the royal couple.

However, there were those who were disgusted with the Pharaoh's public display of love for the common people and mocked him behind his back: 'How could a Pharaoh appear so weak and timid to his subjects, like Akhenaten does?' Others reviled him saying, 'He has not a single trait of his regal father, or proud brother.' Still more looked down on his demeanour: 'Why does he not behave like a pharaoh… why does he not lead his men like pharaohs before him have done for centuries?' Such were the extreme sentiments and emotions that the new Pharaoh aroused among them.

Akhenaten had a penchant for speaking the truth and being outspoken about it. He just could not lie. He would even chide sculptors for making exaggeratedly beautiful features on statues and carvings that they were making of him, like they had done for the erstwhile pharaohs. 'Don't do that,' he told them. 'Your art must portray the truth! All of God's creation should be respected. Please portray me exactly as I am, even if it's not beautiful.'

'But, your Highness, that is not according to tradition,' they lamented.

'It may not be, but I will stand only for the truth to be represented!' Akhenaten was insistent.

In terms of governing his people, Akhenaten banned all forms of punishment. Nobody deserved to be punished; everybody deserved to be loved. He further ordered an end to hostilities with neighbouring lands.

As time went by, Akhenaten had made his discontent with the priests of the temple of Amun – the presiding deity – quite plain. At his coronation, the head priest told him, 'A prince does not become a pharaoh until he is crowned in the temple of Amun.' Akhenaten flatly refused to be crowned there.

'I shall be crowned in the open land under the sunlight, with blessing of the Aten.'

The priests were horrified. They muttered angrily among themselves: 'We don't need a ruler who stays up in darkness and waits for the sun to rise. We need a ruler to stand by us and the traditions which we have upheld for centuries. We are, after all, caretakers of the gods!'

But Akhenaten was of the opinion that all the priests did was to encourage superstition and take advantage of the worshippers so they could fill their own coffers. He could not bear their arrogance, the sway they held over simple people. What's more, he could not understand how people could worship gods they were scared of, gods who wielded enormous power.

He abhorred the authoritarian ways of the priests so much that he issued a decree, which historians say became the chief cause of his downfall. He decreed that all the old temples to other deities be destroyed. In their place would rise new temples in honour of Aten! Such was his love and devotion to Aten that he composed hymns of love and praise to Aten and wanted everyone to experience Aten's love too! Henceforth, Aten was to be the only deity to be worshipped.

A lot of people were happy and danced jubilantly on the streets. But many among them were confused. How could they suddenly stop worshipping the deities their ancestors had been worshipping for generations? They felt the Pharaoh was being insensitive to their beliefs and feelings.

Akhenaten's friends and advisors cautioned him, saying, 'You must allow people to worship whom they choose. Let those who want to worship your 'One and Only God' do so with you, but also let others worship whichever gods they please.' Even the temple priests, livid with the Pharaoh's audacious diktat, backed that suggestion of a compromise because at least it would allow them to stay relevant, and also in business.

However, Akhenaten remained stubborn and refused to budge. His advisors pleaded with him, 'By all means build a temple for your 'One and Only' in every region, but let the other temples remain for those who want to worship the old gods.' But, as it was widely said in those days, it would be easier to move a pyramid, than move Akhenaten from his position.

His childhood friend, disturbed by Akhenaten's obstinacy

and seeing where it could lead, persisted in making him see some sense: 'What sort of an insane, maniacal love is this, Akhenaten? Why force your love and belief onto the people?' Unperturbed, Akhenaten smiled, 'Because I have seen and experienced it for myself. Believe me, dearest friend, it is the only true Love. Do you think I am unaware that this might make me unpopular? I am only doing it out of love for my people; to save them from the clutches of those conniving priests!'

And so, Akhenaten's act, whose noble intention was to spread love, also resulted in spreading hatred and anger among many people and the powerful temple priests. Crime increased as punishment was banned, and the social order broke down. The borders of Egypt became insecure and under imminent threat from ambitious rulers of neighbouring kingdoms who knew only too well that he would have no intentions of going to war. The temple priests began to hatch a devious plot to assassinate Akhenaten.

Accounts of his assassination vary. Some say he was murdered; others say he was made to spend the rest of his days in prison. Subsequent dynasties destroyed the wonderful temples Akhenaten had built in honour of the Aten. All evidence of his reign was obliterated; chiselled away from rock edifices. As far as history was concerned, the misguided poet-Pharaoh was best forgotten.

What couldn't be destroyed was the love that many felt deep in their hearts for him. For his closest friends, Akhenaten was braver than any warrior for he had devoted himself to the service of 'The One and Only', without a thought for the consequences. He had angered the temple priests in order to spread happiness and love. He had fought to spread the message of truth. So great was his love that he did not even judge or punish some of his closest aides who had deserted him to join the enemy camp.

The 'heretic Pharaoh' as he had been dubbed by those against him, was for those who loved him a shining light of a love the likes of which they had never seen before.

Towards the end of his reign, Akhenaten, his heart full of grief, was heard saying aloud to himself, 'Where did I go wrong? After all, I loved everyone from the core of my being. I loved the Aten and carried out the command of 'The One and Only'. Mother, why did things work out this way? But I will always belong to Aten... He will not forsake me.'

At the end of the day, Akhenaten really didn't 'do' anything as such. He followed the voice of his 'One and Only God', the ramifications of which were not in his control. And so did everyone else – each playing their part in this grand story of love and hate. Events played out exactly as they were destined to. Perhaps humanity would be ready for such a love only in the *Satyug* – the Age of Truth.

A tear rolled down Sarah's cheeks. The man waited for her to compose herself. Looking with compassionate eyes, he said:

'Many have shed a tear for Akhenaten's 'insane innocence'. He tried to light up all of Egypt with that love without giving it a choice, just like the earth has no choice but to receive the light of the sun. Many of us can understand the hurt and agony the young prince must have felt at being denied his father's love, because we too have experienced at some time that lack of love in one form or another...'

Sarah looked at him and said, 'I had a valuable insight while you were narrating his story. It reminded me of a specific incident from my childhood, when I was six years old. After that, my father's love for me changed. So, the tears were for both Akhenaten... and me.'

'Yes, but do you get a glimpse – an insight – into how this relates to you today?' he asked.

Sarah looked at him with a puzzled expression.

'Allow me to explain...' he continued.

'All fear, at its very root, is the fear of death. The fear of death of what? Of the 'me'! The 'me' – the 'ego' – is afraid to die. You, as a child, did nothing at first to earn your father's love. You were whole, perfect and pure – pure love, pure spontaneity, pure being. Nothing had to be 'done' by you to earn love. And then, something happened – something totally beyond this child's control, and the child was denied the love of the parent that had until now flowed seamlessly like a gentle river. *What did I do wrong that my father does not love me anymore? What do I have to do to make my father continue loving me?* And thus arose fear: 'What will happen to me without my father's love? I won't be able to live without it. I will cease to exist in his eyes.' In other words, 'I will die.'

So the child then tried to 'do' things to make her father love her, whereas love was her very nature and the very act and effort of 'doing' something was a movement away from that nature.

'So, are you saying..?' Sarah murmured.

'Such is the impact of conditioning, especially in the formative years. The pattern tends to repeat itself as one grows older. As you said, whenever there is a spontaneous attraction between you and a man, the fear arises later and you wonder, 'Will he continue liking me?' In other words, 'What do I have to 'do' to make him continually like me?'

The answer, of course, is 'nothing'. You are whole, perfect, and pure as you are. Nothing need be done as such to retain pure love, for it can never leave. Be who you are – be as you are. You are perfect in spite of the flaws you 'think' you have. In any case, the so-called 'flaws' are only a matter of perception. Next time the fear arises, accept it for what it is – a movement of energy in a body, based on prior conditioning in the formative years. It is not 'my' fear… you didn't instill the fear in yourself in the first place, so why take ownership of it? A 'happening' happened, which resulted in that fear arising. And you had no control over that happening. This way, there is no involvement in the fear, which gives sustenance to the thinking mind of the ego.

Nothing will happen to the true you – the pure being. It is always whole, perfect and pure. Nothing can be added to it, nothing can be taken away from it. It is like the Aten, giving freely of its light to each and everyone, and everything. It is a love without conditions, and giving it is its nature. Whether the 'other' reciprocates that love is a matter for destiny to decide.

As Nisargadatta Maharaj once said: 'In my world love is the only law. I do not ask for love, I give it. Such is my nature.'

Silence prevailed for some minutes until it was interrupted by the bill being presented by the waiter. 'Please allow me to pay the bill,' Sarah said leaning forward to take it. 'I insist, actually. It is my way of saying 'thank you' for the wonderful insight you have given me.'

'Thanking me is like your left hand thanking your right hand,' the man said smiling at her. 'According to

Hindu scriptures, you think that I speak and you listen, but it is Consciousness that does the listening through one instrument, and the speaking through another.'

He got up, bid her a happy farewell, and walked off into the night. She continued to sit at her table for some more time, mulling over the conversation that had taken place, and then left after a while.

That night she had a deep, peaceful sleep. At dawn, shafts of sunlight started streaming through the window and kissed her eyelids which flickered open. She stretched, thinking that it had been very long since she had slept so well. 'Was last evening's conversation with the stranger a dream?' she wondered. She got out of bed with lightness in her heart and walked with a spring in her step to the balcony. Leaning on its rail, she looked up at the sky and a smile lit up her face as the young Pharaoh Amenhotep's words popped into her head:

'Look Mummy, just look at the Aten. See how bright and shining it is... lighting up everything under and around it! Aten makes no distinction between rich and poor, good and bad. It gives life to everything! Aten showers his love equally on everything and everyone.'

She thanked both the Aten and his beloved Akhenaten for the dawn of a new understanding. In that sense, the enlightened Pharaoh's words live on to this day despite the best efforts of subsequent dynasties to eradicate his name from history.

Destiny, as always, has the last and final word.

---

Note: This is a poetic account of the story of Akhenaten. I kept coming across references to the 'heretic Pharaoh' in various books. One book that left its indelible mark was *Akhenaten – Dweller in Truth* by Naguib Mahfouz (Anchor Books). Another book, *Heretic: The life and death of Akhenaten* by Brijit Reed presented me with the idea for this essay.

*'And still, after all this time,*
*the Sun has never said to the Earth,*
*'You owe me.'*
*Look what happens with love like that.*
*It lights up the sky.'*

– Hafez-e Shirazi

# THE WORLD'S BEST ASTROLOGER

I am the world's best astrologer
All that I say comes true
It's bound to happen in your life
So here is my reading for you…

What the next moment brings
You will never ever know
Pleasure or pain, joy or sorrow
Up 'n' down life's roller coaster you will go

Some people will love you
While others you love won't
Sometimes you'll get what you want
But most other times you won't

Bad things seem to happen one after another
The good ones happen now and then
You wonder why bad things happen to good people
For surely they don't deserve them

You'll wonder how a friend bought a swanky car
Though he didn't work half as hard as you did
You'll wish you'd said some words you didn't
And wish you hadn't those which you did

You'll wish your loved ones didn't say
Some of the things that they did
And some of the thing they wouldn't say
You truly wished they did!

You'll lose some people you loved
But what of those you really didn't?
You'll miss those you dearly cherished
But spare a thought for those you didn't

Some friends won't always live up to expectations
And you may not live up to theirs as well
Thoughts of your mortality will keep arising
But in the runaround of daily living they will get quelled

Your concerns will be about health and wealth
For which I have a better cure
Just think for a moment you have no 'body'
And your worries will be over for sure

No 'body' to hate some 'body'
No 'body' to keep you bound
No 'body' to separate you from some 'body'
No 'body' to move around

No 'body' whose health to worry about
No 'body' whose needs to be met
No 'body' to call 'mine' own
And then your life will be better set

After all, it's not all about the 'body'
We realise that we are all here to find
That most elusive treasure of all
Which is called 'peace of mind'

As you grow older, you will have seen
Happy or sad times don't seem to last
'Sic Transit Gloria Mundi...'
Even the glory of the world shall pass

The passing years will help you realise
That the best laid plans often get derailed
You have now learnt the secret of the universe
That God's will always prevails

With this understanding comes
Peace of mind in daily living
An acceptance of 'what is'
While the clock of time goes on ticking

You'll finally sit back and wonder
'How did I go through all that I did?'
And you realise you weren't living your life
That instead you were being lived!

Success and failure, joy and sorrow
Through all of life's dualities
You simply kept flowing
Like a river between life's polarities

You ultimately reach the ocean
Then there's nowhere else to go
For now you have reached 'home'
And you need strive no more

No more do you have to search
For now you are at rest
Peace has come over you now
While life had seemed such a test

Peace is our ultimate destiny
And thank God we must
For in deep sleep we meet it
When all problems turn to dust

Peace is man's eternal quest
The birthright that is his
And get it he does when he realises
'Consciousness is all there is.'

Consciousness is the producer and director
It is the actor and the audience as well
We are instruments through which It functions
May you truly grasp this well

When we are seen for what we truly are
Without the façade of form and name
Then hatred, guilt, jealousy and pride won't arise
And nor will feelings of shame

The same Consciousness functions
Through each and every one
When this understanding cuts through like a knife
It sunders all knots of ill-will at once

When you start living with this understanding
That Consciousness abides in you and me
Then interactions will become meaningful
How much simpler could life be?

For no one truly 'does' anything
It is all the Will of the Source
We are only instruments animated
By the One Divine Force

The future won't frighten you any more
Nor will the past haunt you like before
With the total acceptance of 'what is'
Life will become simpler for sure

All doubts of 'what could have been'
Will disappear without a trace
The planets won't rule over you
For bestowed on you will be Divine Grace

Then on your knees down you will go
Thanking God that all is fine
Moreso when you think of millions suffering
Living below the poverty-line

I am the world's best astrologer
Whatever I say comes true
Although, as God's messenger
I am simply an instrument – just like you

The only message I have for you
Is the one I get from high above
To transcend all obstacles
All you have to be is 'Love'

For love is your true nature,
Nothing more by you need be 'done'
With this attitude in daily living,
All battles will be over before they've begun

Glory be to Consciousness,
That is the One Source
Be still and know this eternal Truth:
Consciousness – true Love – is the Supreme Force

# QUESTIONS & ANSWERS

An interactive Q&A session followed Gautam's talk at Pune in December 2013 on 'The Architecture of Daily Living'.

Here are some excerpts...

*Q. I have often heard the word 'Choicelessness' being mentioned by people who are on the spiritual path. What exactly is choicelessness?*

A. By 'Choicelessness', it is meant that one's choice itself is 'choiceless'. This is because what you think is your choice, is truly not 'your' choice. Your choice is based on your genes and conditioning – two factors over which you had no control. Choicelessness does not mean that you don't choose – let's say, blue or green. It means that you choose what is in your nature to choose.

'Choice' means you have the ability to make and take a decision. I have to decide whether to take a left or a right turn on the road – that is my free will and my choice. The average person thinks that it is 'my will' which is making me take the left or right turn. But, in truth, there are a lot of factors that determine your decision, and these factors are not in your control.

You all may feel that it is your will that made you come here, but the fact is that if I had not written a book, and if Khushru (the organiser) had not read it, I would not have been invited for this talk. Further, if I were not a publisher – my book probably wouldn't have got published.

*(Laughter)*

If that stream of events had not happened, I would not be here with you today.

Similarly, how much of 'your will' did you exercise to come here? It's possible that you may not have been on the mailing list and, therefore, not seen the announcement of the talk. You could have got stuck in traffic, or another engagement could have come up. So do you see the chain of events, which goes far back, that influences what you decide to do at some later date? Yet you feel it's one action of 'mine' that is 'my choice'.

Day to day living requires one to make and take decisions. One has to because that is how we, as human beings, function – by taking decisions. All I am saying is that you must remember that the outcome of your decision is not in your control, because the outcome will be according to God's will. What's more, don't indulge in 'what ifs' and blame yourself: 'If I had not done that, then this wouldn't have happened,' and so on. Don't blame yourself because what you thought was your free will was truly not your free will.

*Q. Can you illustrate this by some example, if possible?*

A. In the Bhagavad Gita, Arjuna saw the enemy's entire army positioned against him, whereas on his part, he had chosen only Krishna. So he told Krishna, 'I can fight my relatives,

QUESTIONS & ANSWERS

but I cannot fight my preceptors,' and having said that he put his bow and quiver of arrows down. Krishna said, 'Look here, you were born in the warrior caste, your whole training in life has been to be a warrior, you are designed to fight... so you pick up that bow and fight because that is your dharma. And please don't think you are killing them, because I – as Time – have already killed them.'

One day at my guru Ramesh's home, a man of around 65 years of age came for the talks. He had been a veteran soldier somewhere in Europe. He said that for every night since the end of the war, he had broken down in tears because he had killed some soldiers of the enemy. And Ramesh told him the same thing. He said, 'Look, you belong to a family of soldiers (the man had said even his grandfather was a soldier), you were conscripted into the military when you were a young boy, your conditioning was to fight for the country, so why are you taking ownership of the fact that you killed the enemy? If you realise that you were meant to kill, then you will be at peace.' And this man just started sobbing. He said, 'I am now ready to die tomorrow.' So, let's not become attached to what we think is our choice and free will. Not being attached is a liberating feeling.

Hitler was born because it was God's will, and so was Osama Bin Laden. By 'God' I mean the Source or Consciousness, and not an individual sitting up there in heaven. If God did not create 'bad' people, then who created them? There cannot be two 'Sources', otherwise it would beget the question that where did they come from? The Source created Hitler, and the Source created Mother Teresa.

Consciousness does not differentiate. One of the more painful facets of humanity is that of handicapped children

149

and you wonder how God could do that. God would probably answer that by saying, 'Nobody asks Me why I created healthy children!' We don't know the basis of God's will. The Nirbhaya case (someone in the audience had raised the issue of the recent gang rape that had created a mass revolution of sorts in India) is horrific. But what it does to each of us, how each of us is impacted individually, how we are impacted collectively as a group, what it makes us feel – in other words, what role that event was supposed to play, will be played according to God's will.

When Jesus said while he was nailed to the cross: 'Not my will Oh Lord, but Thine,' that signified his total surrender to God's will.

Now, as far as the perpetrators of the Nirbhaya rape were concerned, thankfully they were all nabbed and the law of the land will take its course. What punishment the Court metes out to them would ultimately be God's will. Just as it was God's will that they be nabbed. A happening may be God's will, but it does not absolve the individual of the consequences of his action and his responsibility to society – which is also God's will.

*Q. This kind of approach can be perceived as fatalistic, and it can border on inaction.*

A. Do exactly what you think and feel you should do, but know that the results of your action are not in your control. This does not mean 'sit back'. It's not in your nature to sit back. Fatalism is felt by the ego – it feels helpless with this approach. It does not like it. But it's not that. Deep down, the arrow has hit home. With this approach, you will be more relaxed when you do things. You will not be that attached, you will still do them but there will be a lightness because you know that, in any case, the results are not in your control. It will not make you fatalistic; you will, in fact, enjoy doing those things much more than you did before. Why? Because it will no longer be 'you' doing them. You have the realisation that it is happening through you.

As the famous Russian ballet dancer Nidjinsky once said: 'Nidjinsky dances best when Nidjinsky is not there.'

Q. *Could Advaita be perceived as the lazy man's guide to life and living?*

A. A 27-year young man, who was impacted by the teaching, once said to me, 'I am not in 'thinking mind' mode; I play video games all the time so I am in 'working mind' mode.' What he meant to say was that he was not sitting idle but keeping his mind engaged. Then he went on to say, 'It's my destiny to play video games and not to work,' and so on.

See, the ego is very naughty. At the heart of the matter was the burning question: 'Who am I without 'my' mind?' It was afraid of that, because it felt it would lose its identity, its sense of self, if the mind was not kept engaged in some activity or another.

You could call it a cunning or conniving mind, but the beauty is that it was made that way. So you can't tell someone 'You have a conniving mind.' That is your interpretation. God made that person that way for a reason. His spiritual growth would happen when he would realise that nature of the ego. So this young man, even if one says he has a conniving mind, the realisation should be there that he is not a conniving 'being'. How can a human being be conniving? A 'being' can simply 'be' – being. There's a big difference between the two statements. It is the nature of the mind to be conniving. If you start looking at people from that perspective, you will be more relaxed. The resonance of the intellect is in the heart, not in the mind. We should think from the heart, and not the mind.

This does not mean you should not tell someone – let's say your son (pointing at a couple who said their teenage son was giving them a hard time) – to stop playing video games throughout the day, if that's what arises. You should not prevent what comes naturally to you as well. But deep down you know that you're not targeting an individual 'me' but a person programmed by his genes and conditioning – both factors that are beyond his control. So it removes the sting from your relationship with people.

*(On the same couple's earlier question regarding the difficult time their son was giving them.)*

It's the way their ego is conditioned – by your upbringing of them, which plays a large part in the child's conditioning. One also has to take into account the conditioning they receive in school, college, society in general, and so on.

*Q. But, what do I do when my son uses that same argument with me when confronted?*

A. The fact is that you were not responsible, because God was responsible for your conditioning. So, the next time it happens you might laugh, because you will realise that he is playing out a script based on his destiny. He is meant to think the way he is thinking, and you are meant to be there to put forward your point of view. But his problem is that you keep repeating your point of view.

See, the ego never likes to be told the same thing over and over again. He will rebel against that. All you need to do is plant the seed, and then let go of constantly trying to put someone on a particular path. It's just like constantly watering the seed which would destroy it, instead of giving it the time and environment to sprout and grow. You know, our mother never once said 'No' to us. And because of that, all of us siblings grew up quite well-disciplined. So, the next time when you see that that's the way the person's mind is working, you will perhaps give a quiet smile of understanding.

*Q. The thing is that he wants to come closer but there's something holding him back. I know it's a matter of time, it will happen when it's supposed to happen, but if one wants to hasten that process, what does one do?*

A. Doing something about that would mean a lot of 'doership' on your part. He wants to come closer to you because of who you are. So, by going out of your way to do something in order to make that person come closer, you are, in a sense, going away from your own centre. It will be the destiny of that person who is attracted to you, to come to you. And his journey lies in that journey towards you. I would say you have to be exactly as you are. So, if the ego steps in and wants to hasten things, that would create a disturbance in the dynamic – of course, if that happened, then even that would be destined. There is something in you that is wanting the other person to come to you; just remain a witness to that. Investigate those moments – what is your state which is drawing him to you? Be present for him as That.

The best thing that you can do is to just witness.

However, the point is that witnessing is not something you can 'do'. Witnessing happens when the sense of doership is not there. 'Witnessing' is not the same as 'observing' because when we observe, we judge. Observing is the 'me' observing something else done by the individual. When you are impartial and have not established a point of view, it is then that witnessing happens. The ego cannot try to witness because the ego, as the thinking mind, is not the witness. Witnessing is the total collapse of the thinking mind, which is the characteristic of the ego, into the total acceptance of this present moment.

*Q. So does this mean that the whole game is that the ego wants to survive with its story, its attachment to certain feelings and pleasures, and the witness has to watch this game?*

A. The witness is that which is aware of this happening. So when the awareness arises that 'I am in a game', that is the witness. The more the awareness that you are in a game – the *lila*, the more the witnessing is happening.

*Q. Sometimes the game gets very intense and one forgets...*

A. That's the flip-flop. But with time that starts reducing. It's like climbing a hundred steps... one at a time. Life is a learning curve. With this understanding, your involvement in situations starts reducing. Your drama is playing out in consciousness. If you were not conscious, there would be no drama being played out. So, the teaching is just pointing you back to the consciousness, which is the witness. You can't have a problem with someone if you are not conscious. In deep sleep, you cannot have a problem with anyone.

*Q. What about getting bored?*

A. Boredom is natural, else one wouldn't get bored. If that is destined to happen, it will happen. Who is it that gets bored? Sit with the boredom once. Don't avoid it by becoming engaged in other things. One type of boredom is an energetic boredom where the body needs to walk, exercise, and expend energy in order for the feeling to go away. But more often than not, boredom is in the mind. And one tries to engage in other activities so one does not get bored. In a sense, one is running away from just 'being'.

For example, some people have a hard time sitting in meditation with their eyes closed. They get bored. That is because they are habituated to being engaged in something or the other – they are externalised. Then there are others who just close their eyes and are lost to the world. No one gets bored in meditation – it's the mind that gets bored. Why? Because the mind wants to survive, it does not want to die. In meditation it dies.

Real meditation is Consciousness contemplating on Itself. Thoughts are witnessed just like traffic moving by. There is no attachment to these thoughts, which normally translates into thinking. Thoughts will arise, because that is the nature of thoughts. You can't block a thought. Here, thoughts are not the issue, but rather, thinking is. It is the stretching out of a thought in the duration of time that is the issue.

When you're comfortable with just being, you will realise that you don't have to be 'doing' all the time. Boredom could be a sign that the person is habituated to the 'doing' mode all the time. You could not 'do' if you were not conscious. And meditation is Consciousness contemplating on Itself. Meditation is making one realise that Consciousness is one's true nature.

*Q. But doesn't meditation cause the mind – the thinking mind – to go all over the place? And you can't actually do anything about it?*

A. In meditation, you are aware that your mind is going all over the place. In the waking state you are not aware. So be happy that a lot of thoughts come in meditation because you are aware that they are there. Most of us are not aware; we are just caught up in running here and there with our thoughts. The fact that you said a lot of thoughts come during meditation means you were not those thoughts and, therefore, you recognised them as thoughts. People get discouraged when they realise they get a lot of thoughts in meditation, but that's actually very good. The thought does not occur: 'Who knows that?' Who knows that there are many thoughts coming? With time, the thinking will subside in meditation. In life we are constantly taught the same lessons in order to bring them to our awareness. Once we learn something, it generally does not manifest again because the learning is complete. Your head is already in the tiger's mouth, as the first step of sitting in meditation has already been taken.

*Q. In one of your books it is written: 'Read the Bhagavad Gita from the perspective of Krishna.' What do you mean by that?*

A. That is what the sage Nisargadatta Maharaj used to say. His whole teaching was that 'you are not the body'. So what he is saying is, don't read the Gita from an individual perspective. Read it as if you are 'the pure light of Consciousness reading the book'. In other words, if you were not conscious, you could not read the Gita. So read it from that perspective and not from the twisted judgements and views of the individual 'me' – an individual identified with the name and form of his body. Read it from the perspective of the Universal Consciousness – Krishna. Do not read it from the perspective of the identified ego consciousness.

Q. *Then that should go for anything and everything, shouldn't it?*

A. If you can live like that, then that is 'awakened' living. If you are free from resentments, ill-will, spite, hatred, jealousy, pride, arrogance, guilt and shame – the game is up. But if you *think* you are free from all that, then the game is not up.
*(Laughter)*

Q. *When a deer sees a lion, it is afraid and automatically runs away. Isn't the deer afraid of death?*

A. Of course it is. The deer is programmed to be afraid of biological death, so it runs.

Q. *Well, so am I!*

A. No. You ask questions, which the deer does not. The deer does not live in fear – fear of the future. Unlike you, he does not think: 'What's going to be my bank balance three years from now?' ...and so on. The biological fear of death in a human being is that which does not make you close your eyes and cross the road. That is what is common between the deer and a human being. But we have a psychological problem with dying. We have the intellect that God gave us, which makes us ask questions. The deer has no questions to ask. The deer does not want possessions, it does not build a monumental story around another deer it falls in love with – 'Will you be with me for the rest of my life?' – nor does it indulge in other such projections.

*Q. But the deer also falls in love and has children…*

A. That's a natural, biological process – pure being. The deer does not seek permanency in the future.

*Q. What about nomads?*

A. They're probably more 'awakened' than most of us. They don't get attached to places and things. They simply move on. We get habituated even to which restaurants we go to, and which table we sit at.
    *(Laughter)*

*Q. Would you elaborate on the concept of God?*

A. For most of us, God is an object – one which we pray to. More often than not, that prayer is in the form of begging, asking God to do this or that for us. That is not the God being referred to. The God being referred to is Consciousness. If you were not conscious, you could not worship any God. So who are you referring to when you say God? Is it the God that is within your consciousness as an object? Or the Consciousness within which is the object one calls God? Some people don't like the word 'God' because of a lot of conditioning associated with it, so 'Consciousness' is a more appropriate word. It is the Source without which there is nothing – no 'you', 'me', 'he' or 'she'.

Q. *But you say there is a plan, and it's working according to His will.*

A. Well, it's not working according to your will. If it did, then everything you did in life would go your way. So, it is working according to the will of the Source.

Q. *But the Source resides in you, right?*

A. The Source does not reside in you; it is you who reside in the Source.
*(Laughter)*
We actually got disconnected from the Source, because it was the will of the Source. The Source wants to reconnect to Itself through us.

Q. *Then why do you use the words 'God' and 'Source'? Why not use the word 'Consciousness'?*

A. Because if I keep using the word Consciousness, my tongue will get tired.
*(Laughter)*

Q. *Some people don't like the concept of God.*

A. You know, my teacher used to say that an atheist can be an atheist only if it is 'God's will'.
*(Laughter)*
On a more serious note, if he was not conscious he would not be an atheist. So the teaching keeps pointing back to Consciousness.

*Q. Does denying God mean that there is a God to deny?*

A. Obviously. That is the first sign of God. The sage Ramana Maharshi once told his audience: 'There is no free will.' One person put up his hand and said, 'I put up my hand, so that's my free will.' Sri Ramana said: 'Of course not! If I had not said that there is no free will, you would not have put up your hand!'

*Q. What tools would you recommend to the audience to lessen this duality, to be less fragmented?*

A. No tools. Who wants the tools? The mind – more specifically, the thinking mind! So please don't get involved in trying to be a witness, because the ego cannot witness.

## Questions asked through email

*Q. Nisargadatta Maharaj said that one has to be convinced that he is not the body. In one particular talk, he said: 'Like a body is being cremated, it is gone. You have to be convinced like that.' Is the conviction of not being the body sufficient to stop the cycle of birth and death? Or does one have to realise the Self… and awaken?*

A. According to my understanding, the conviction that you are not the body is the 'awakening'. It is the Total Conviction, and not just an intellectual conviction.

After this, there is no 'one' to be concerned with the cycle of birth and death.

Q. *I am currently reading your book 'Explosion of Love' and have also recently read Ramesh's 'Peace and Harmony in Daily Living'. The teaching of Advaita resonates deeply with me, and I often experience a deep peace and contentment, mostly when I am alone or in nature and relax into my being, not thinking.*

*However, I have a question that I have been struggling with. The teachings I am reading seem to say 'don't fight one's conditioning' and 'it's all the Divine will, whatever happens is meant to happen'.*

*I was brought up by a father who was an alcoholic and also abusive, and a mother that passively went along with the situation.*

*I learnt the patterns of my mother and father growing up, and continued to act out various patterns until my early 30s when life seemed to stop working for me: relationships broke down, jobs did not work out, I felt angry, depressed, empty, alone.*

*I am now 38 years of age and have been working on my emotional and psychological health, and my spiritual understanding. But I am tired, very tired, of the therapy, yoga classes, health treatments, healers, etc. I seem to oscillate between the stress and work of trying to 'de-condition' myself, and the unhealthy ways of thinking and acting that seem to be the default. I can understand that. 'Self-improvement' can be an exhausting process.*

A. Indeed, that was your childhood conditioning, over which you had no control. And neither did your father and mother over their conditioning. That is the Advaita perspective.

At a talk given by me last year, a man asked me that he had tried various healings and therapies – reiki, pranic healing, workshops, courses and so on, and he was quite a spiritual tourist in that sense. He wondered if and when this would stop, as he had been at it for over 20 years.

My answer was simple. I said that it would stop the moment he asked himself what he was looking for. Once he knew that, then at least he would know whether he found it. He was quite astonished. He said he did not know what he was looking for, and even the thought of it had not arisen.

Then I repeated what my guru used to say: 'What the human being is looking for deep down, and whether he knows it or not, is peace of mind.' The fact that he was continuing 'looking around' meant he had not found that elusive peace of mind. This impacted him tremendously as he wholeheartedly agreed that it was peace of mind that he was looking for. He now knows that there is a 'criteria' and he needn't look around aimlessly.

Sometimes, one has the good fortune of chancing upon the teaching of Advaita, which in my experience is capable of bestowing this peace. You have said that it resonates deeply within you. That is because it validates your life experience.

We did not create our childhood conditioning in the first place, and yet we get involved in endless efforts to 'de-condition' our conditioning. It is ironic, but that is the way the ego functions – in a mode based on 'doership'. Advaita offers a unique perspective in its understanding. This is what is meant by 'don't fight one's conditioning'. When it is clearly seen that we are all products of our genes and conditioning, both of which are not in our control, then how can we blame others (and more importantly, ourselves) for something they or we are supposed to have done?

We are all instruments through whom God's will functions. When this realisation sinks deeper and deeper, it is observed that one's conditioning gets transformed over a period of time; sometimes it gets transformed instantly. So, rather than 'doing' something to de-condition oneself, it is in fact the Understanding that starts working through you, in daily living. This in turn creates fresh conditioning, and it is reflected in one's attitude and response to current situations. All we need to 'do' is give it a chance. In other words, your resonation with Advaita *is* the new conditioning that brings you the peace.

*Q. I find peace only when I am alone, away from the city, feeling safe and close to nature. This, however, is very hard to sustain because one needs to earn money to live, and one also desires contact with other human beings. How can this be achieved?*

A. Yes, peace is found more easily when one is amidst nature or when one is alone as there are no others to deal with. That is, no other 'egos' to deal with. However, daily living involves relationships with others – be they friends, relatives or strangers. And peace of mind in 'daily living' is what is sought, which is the precious gift of Advaita.

As you rightly say, one needs to earn money to live and one also desires contact with other human beings. I would encourage you to go back and take another dip in the waters of daily living, rather than isolating yourself, as you have been gifted with this teaching.

*Q. My question is simply this: If one's conditioning leads one to do harm to oneself and others, but Advaita says not to fight the conditioning, is this my karma/destiny?*

A. I don't think it is a question of 'fighting' the conditioning, which perhaps is something you might have been doing through your spiritual practices. I repeat, Advaita brings to awareness that your actions are a result of your genes and conditioning, over neither of which you have any control. This makes it easier to accept others, as well as yourself, for who they or you are. Acceptance of 'what is' makes one see things in a clearer, impersonal light. That awareness, and how deeply it sinks in (even if initially only at the intellectual level), can itself change, alter or transform the current conditioning. Who is the one concerned with 'fighting' the conditioning? It's the ego, of course, which can only do things like 'fight', as it derives its sense of self from that very activity.

Destiny is 'what is' in the moment. And one never knows what the next moment brings. Why project the past into the future and wonder whether that's your destiny? It is the 'thinking mind' which tends to do that. Why assume you may do harm to yourself or others as part of your destiny, based on past experience? Let God decide that.

My guru would always say to seekers who came to visit him: 'Why consider your glass half empty? Consider it half full. If God has brought you here so far, why think that he will drop you here?' Perhaps you need to take a break from trying to de-condition yourself, and let life flow with the new perspective you have gained.

Further, if there is a deep understanding, then the issue of harming others would not arise. If there is the deep understanding that it is the same Consciousness that functions through all of us, where is the question of harming someone for something they are supposed to have 'done'?

That is all I have to offer for now. May you rest in the warm embrace of the teaching.

✓

*Q. Does 'oneness' mean that I will live everyone else's life? The idea that everyone around me is really just 'me' is highly disturbing.*

A. Consciousness functions through different human beings like electricity functions through different household appliances. Just as the electrical juicer is programmed to produce a different output from the toaster, similarly each individual body-mind organism is programmed differently – as a result of genetics and conditioning – to produce a specific output. We are instruments through whom the same energy functions.

Therefore, to answer your question, 'everyone is really me' in the sense that it is the same Consciousness that functions through the different 'me's. However, each 'me' lives his life as a separate 'me'. Therefore, the question of living another 'me's' life does not arise, just as the juicer cannot perform the same function as the toaster.

At a deeper level of understanding, it means that Consciousness is all there is; there truly are no others to be separate from. We are not living our lives but rather are *being lived*, just as the gadgets in the kitchen are being lived by the electricity that functions through them.

## An email correspondence from an aspirant seeking clarity

*ND: I am not sure why I am writing this to you and whether you would reply.*

*I am restless. Reading books and browsing videos of spiritual masters seems to have become a habit, an obsession. Some say there is nothing to be done; others say something must be done.*

*To look for the sense of 'I am' is what I try to do these days, but I am not sure if that is the way for me.*

*'Is there a need for the presence of a teacher?' This question is bothering me. I am not even sure if I truly have the desire to understand myself, or is it just an escape from daily problems?*

*I stumbled upon your videos today and thought you might know what really is going on, and help me.*

*I will be grateful if I can get a pointer from you.*

GS: What you have stated is the plight of many spiritual seekers. The consolation (for you) is that you did not start the seeking in the first place; God did. So let the path unfold as per His plan.

Generally, what I have observed is that such confusion arises because we don't know what we are looking for. But it is clear that what every human being is looking for, whether he knows it or not, is 'peace of mind'.

Therefore, I would suggest following that path or finding a teacher who shows you the way to attain 'peace of mind' in daily living. For what could be more important than that?

The point you raised in your mail is important: 'I am not even sure if I truly have the desire to understand myself or is it just an escape from daily problems?' The truth is that only you would know whether you are escaping from daily problems, or whether you are facing them but, at the same time, also seeking a balm (in the form of a teacher or teaching) that will help you face such situations with equanimity.

I can't say whether the presence of a teacher would be 'essential' in your case, but I am sure it would help the process. I was in the physical presence of my teacher and for me it was essential. I think it was essential for my teacher as well (i.e. to be with his teacher).

All the best for the unfolding of your spiritual journey – it is something to be enjoyed. Consider your glass half full and not half empty.

*ND: As suggested by you, I contemplated on what I really want. I am convinced now that it is the search for 'peace of mind' and may be happiness. But peace of mind, a feeling of being content, seems to resonate more.*

*So far, my main motive was to achieve the feeling of being someone special. I am now probably clearer about what it was, and what it is.*

*Writing to you about the confusion in my mind helped put me at ease. I am now more convinced that things are happening, and that I am not the one who is making them happen.*

*Thank you so much for being there for me.*

GS: 'Peace of mind' is the true happiness as it is not a happiness that depends on momentary pleasures.

Yes, the ego indeed wants to be special. That has now been seen clearly.

Thanking me is like your left hand thanking your right hand.

*ND: It has been some time since I last wrote to you.*

*Moments of silence are happening to me these days. Sometimes, when I am trying to be one with the feeling of 'I am', I can't seem to do it. My mind goes on chattering. However, at times the silence pops up spontaneously.*

*Sometimes, in that silence, my attention gets locked on to some part of the brain, the forehead, the right side of brain or on my nose. Though I try to move it or unlock it, I cannot seem to consciously do it. After some time my focus, or attention, seems to go off on its own.*

*I do not understand what it is, why it is, and how to deal with it.*

*Could you please say something about it?*

GS: Like you have said, when you try to be one with the 'I am', you can't do it. That's precisely the point. It is this very 'you' with its sense of 'doership' that tries too hard to be its own absence, so that the 'Presence' shines through. Yes, the 'silence' indeed pops up spontaneously without you having to do anything.

Now, regarding the experience of your attention getting locked on to some part of the brain: as long as it happens on its own, without you trying to induce it, let it play its part in the process of unfoldment. As you have said, it goes off on its own after some time. The Creative Force has infinite intelligence and does not require 'you' to 'do' anything with it; it will take its natural course.

*ND: Thank you. I could not have shared all this with anyone else. I feel really blessed to have your guidance. I can now see that the trying itself prevents the 'silence'.*

*When the mind is very active and there is no sense of separation from it, then I feel very frustrated. What would be the best course of action at such time?*

*Also, I never used to wake up early. Since the past week, there is an urge to wake up early in the morning and sit in silence. I feel like doing this even in the evening. On my way home from office, I have found a quiet place in a garden, where I can sit and contemplate. This appears strange even to me, but I am doing it. I will continue doing it as long as there is the urge.*

*I will keep reporting further such happenings to you.*

GS: When the mind is very active, one can only hope that the understanding comes forth and cuts off the involvement. To 'do' anything to cut off the involvement would mean getting 'involved' in the involvement.

Many people underrate the value of sitting in silence, but it is the best practice. It is nice to know that it is 'happening' for you. As you said, continue doing it until the urge is there.

*ND: Thank you for taking the time out of your busy schedule to reply. You have been very kind to me.*

*I want to tell you about the experience I had today; I am hesitant, because I don't know if it was really happening. I was doing something but there was also an internal dialogue going on about what I am and who the 'me' really is, and all that.*

*I happened to look at the wall in front of me and, somehow, I felt that I was hollow inside – meaning that there was nothing inside me. I felt that the wall in front of me and my body were in a field of something, and they were both appearing in that field. I felt that there was some distance between the wall and me, but I was not sure if it can really be called a 'distance'.*

*Everything had a jelly-like texture. It was not feeling solid. But when I touched the wall, I could feel it was solid to the touch. There was also something inside me saying, 'What is this happening? Is there nothing in my brain as 'me'? Does this mean my mind is 'empty' now?'*

*I am now confused. Was this kind of made up by my mind because I have been reading or hearing about it? But surely, I can't be mistaking that feeling.*

*Can you please guide me?*

GS: What you have described is known as 'witnessing'. The fact that you say, 'I was doing something and also internal dialogue was going on about what is me' and all that... means that there was awareness of it all. In other words, all phenomena were witnessed.

The world is not out there; it appears within our consciousness. For if we were not conscious, there would be no world.

Sitting in silence for some time and meditation – which is the simple awareness of being – would be beneficial.

Witnessing means observing all that arises – thoughts, feelings, emotions – without judging.

*ND: I was eagerly waiting for your response.*

*More things are unfolding since last week and I am feeling so much gratitude. It's almost like I am thanking everything and everyone around for what has been happening.*

*I was not sure what that experience was when I wrote to you but now, with your confirmation, I can say that things are happening as they are meant to happen. Right now when I write this, my mind is almost switched off. If it can happen to me, no word other than 'grace' comes to my mind to explain it. It happens at its will and I can only witness it, and thank it.*

*I do not know what is going to happen next, but I am now sure that it will be what it has to be.*

*I want to remain in silence because I cannot explain to anyone else what is happening. Probably this is how it is supposed to happen.*

GS: Gratitude to God is perhaps the only genuine prayer. Wanting to thank everyone and everything around you is akin to thanking God – for God, or Consciousness, is all there is.

Grace is indeed the right word.

*'When the sense of
distinction and separation
is absent,
you may call it love.'*

– Sri Nisargadatta Maharaj

# AFTERWORD

Life is but a 'blip' that appears on the screen of the Consciousness that is not aware of Itself. What is born is 'I am' – Consciousness now aware of Itself. Shiva has become Shiva-Shakti.

Death is the end of the blip that appears on the screen of Consciousness, signifying the end of 'I am'. 'We' go back to what we were before we were born – Consciousness not aware of Itself.

When we refer to 'our' future, what future are we truly talking about? Our future is ultimately going back to the same state we were in before we were born. So, are we really going into the future, or are we going back to the past?

All we are doing is reversing into the future, for that is where we came from.

## The beginning of separation

In life, the 'I am' – the impersonal awareness of simply 'being', gets identified with a name and form as a separate entity at around the age of 1½ to 2 years. Thus the ego is born, and the illusion of separation begins. The ego – the thinking mind – believes it is separate from others, just as a wave is separate from other waves. But it really doesn't matter as the content of the wave, as with all waves, is water. The source of the wave – be it a small one or a tidal wave – is the still depth of the ocean; the wave itself being a temporary phenomenon on the surface that eventually merges back into the ocean. In other words, stillness is the wave's real nature, even when it appears as a wave in motion. The destiny of the wave is to finally return to where it came from – to merge with its source.

## The end of separation

Death, then, can truly only refer to the death of the body. Consciousness is all there is, whether as the Unmanifest Absolute, the impersonal consciousness in the deep sleep state, or the identified consciousness in the dream and waking states. There is no question of death for Consciousness – for It was never born. It always IS.

The illustration on the next page illustrates the merging of the individual consciousness with the Source Consciousness at the moment of death of the body. It was one of the visions received by my mother in her meditations, which was part of the process of her spiritual unfoldment that began with the question: 'Who am I? Where do I come from? Where do I go?'

## The final expansion

*'A beam of light extends from the Ajna chakra (third eye), tracing a path up towards the forehead for consciousness to move out through the centre of the head. It is seen piercing the cosmos, creating a ripple, and merging with the Source Consciousness. While it is doing this, all the chakras, at different centres of the body, start unwinding, expanding, and merging with their respective elements.*

*What keeps rotating is a subtle form resembling the Yin Yang symbol at the level of the Manipur chakra.'* *

---

* *Kundalini Awakening* – Santosh Sachdeva, Yogi Impressions. Illustration reproduced with permission.

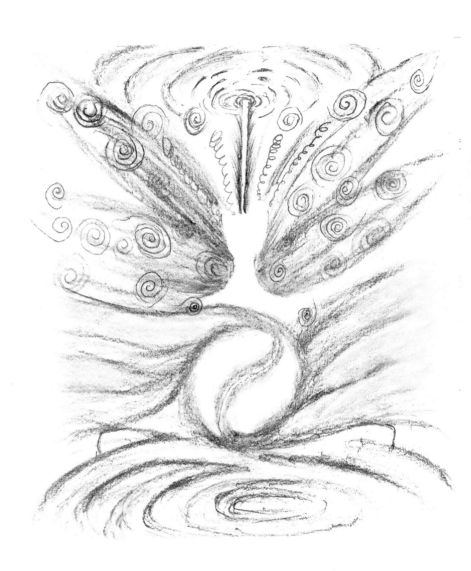

APPENDIX

## REFLECTION ON
## 'PATTERNS: THE CRY OF THE EGO'
(A note by integral psychotherapist Dr. Sonera Jhaveri)

Gautam's essay very coherently defines and delineates what our unconscious, automatic and habitual behaviours are. As he very correctly states, 'Patterns are created without the ego's conscious involvement.' Patterns, both positive and negative, stem from the past either through nurturing or disturbing emotional experiences, respectively.

Through the observation of other peoples' self oblivion (of their patterns), the essay reflects on the relationship between psychology and spirituality, more specifically in this context, the relationship to Advaita Vedanta. In a real sense, there is no binary opposition between doing psychological work and undertaking a spiritual inquiry as they are both at different ends of the same existential spectrum of life. Psychological work is a very important precursor to spiritual work, as it is our psychological wounds that hinder us from advancing on the spiritual path.

The sufferings and injuries from the past keep us in a state of contraction and unconsciousness. This happens because we develop defences around our past traumas and often these are then embodied as unconscious patterns. Since patterns are always at the edge of awareness, they reflect focal areas in our lives where we are self-blind, which in essence are the key areas of psychotherapeutic work.

Depth psychology has much to say about patterns. They represent what Jung has called the 'shadow' or disowned aspects of the self, which we do not want to recognise in us and are often projected on to others. When it is under the spell of its shadow, the ego often thinks that it's always 'others who are angry, jealous, empathetic, speak loudly or rudely, while I am not like that'. As Gautam mentions in his essay, if we think others are jealous then we have also been jealous ourselves and hence judge the other for being 'jealous'.

When one is unconscious of one's patterns, one is prone to what Freud called 'repetition compulsion' which, very briefly, is the human propensity to repeat unproductive and even self-harmful behaviours *ad nauseum*, so as to keep ourselves in a space of psycho-emotional familiarity. Through the repetition of automatic thoughts, beliefs, assumptions and behaviours, patterns take form and through them we construct our own subjectivities.

Our personalities then, in effect, are the constellations of our different patterns that are generally organised around what is known and what we are used to – for better or worse. For instance, if a girl grew up with an unavailable father she might take that unavailability as a sign of love and will, unconsciously, be drawn to unavailable romantic partners later in life.

Contemporaneously, from the perspective of neuroscience, our patterns literally get entrenched in our neural architecture as the way we habitually behave and react determines the way the neurons in our brain 'fire and wire together'. These, in turn, create neural pathways that get activated when the slightest environmental trigger is present and predisposing us to act out our patterns. For example, initially someone gets angry when they are made uncomfortable over big things like being harassed. Over time, the tolerance to being uncomfortable becomes less and less and one will blow up at the smallest of irritations, like someone knocking a glass down at the dinner table by mistake.

How do we then work and deconstruct our patterns? Both psychotherapy and Advaita Vedanta offer us a way by respectively articulating the Observing Ego or the Self in Advaita Vedanta that does not identify with passing mental phenomena. It is only through conscious self-observation and witnessing that we can emancipate our selves from our patterns, as we are then able to recognise and dis-identify with them and not act them out. Gautam's six pointers at the end of the essay are a good place to begin reflecting on one's own unconscious patterns, and how one can deconstruct and emancipate oneself from these patterns.

To conclude, both psychotherapeutic work and Advaita Vedanta would concur that the patterns one embodies should be seen as 'a' pattern and not 'my' pattern, however, they differ on the understanding, orientation and capabilities of the human ego.

Psychotherapeutic work is based on the premise that the Observing Ego is not only capable of having an awareness of a pattern, but also of taking self-responsibility for it and changing it, granting the subject a maturing of the ego. Advaita Vedanta discredits the ego's awareness and highlights the non-doership of the Self, taking the self-observational process onto a transcendental level. Yet, whether the ego can or cannot have awareness is a point of semantics, since there is a deep observational core in every human subjectivity – whether it is called the Observing Ego or Atman remains a redundant difference.

– Dr. Sonera Jhaveri

M.Sc. - London (LSE), M.Sc. - London (UCL)
M.A. & Ph.D. - California Institute of Integral Studies

Dr. Jhaveri has a private practise in Mumbai. She is also a mental health consultant at Nanavati Hospital, Mumbai.

# ACKNOWLEDGEMENTS

God has showered me with more grace than I probably deserve for giving me and my sisters the most wonderful parents. A mother who has been a guiding light not only for us, but also for those who have accepted her as their guru, mentor and guide. And a father who, during the short time he was with us, imbued and ingrained the values that have stood us in good stead.

I would also like to express deep gratitude to my spiritual teacher, the late Ramesh Balsekar, for his grace and blessings that are always with me.

And to those spiritual guides whom it has been a privilege to know: Justice M. L. Dudhat, Eckhart Tolle, Master Charles Cannon, and Yogiraj Siddhanath.

It has been my good fortune to work together with many wonderful beings on this book. My thanks to:

My mother Santosh, always the first one to go through my writings.

My sisters Shibani and Nikki for their unconditional support all along.

Shiv Sharma, for pruning the essays and for his insightful editorial inputs.

Gary Roba, for offering whole-hearted support in going through the writings and making pertinent suggestions. He is always such a pleasure to work together with.

Gabriel Halfon, to whom I would send across the essays as and when they were written, for his honest and encouraging feedback.

Sonera Jhaveri (Psychotherapist), Samira Amin (Counsellor), and Meena Kapur (Psychotherapist), for their valuable inputs on the essay, *Patterns: The Cry of the Ego*.

Khushru Irani, Richard Syrop and Natasha Gupta, for helping with the proof-reading.

Girish Jathar and Sanjay Malandkar for the layout and DTP.

Priya Mehta for the book design, and Devika Khanna for her input.

The team at Yogi Impressions, for all their hard work in steering the ship successfully.

Nikhil Kripalani, Sheetal Sanghvi, Khushru Irani, Heiner Siegelmann, Christiane Persson and Ludmila Kotomina, who in their respective ways have helped spread the teaching.

All the readers and those who have written to me over the years, thank you for giving me the opportunity to share what I have learnt along the journey of life.

For information on Gautam Sachdeva, visit:
www.gautamsachdeva.com

The author may be contacted on email:
mails@gautamsachdeva.com

For further details, contact:
**Yogi Impressions Books Pvt. Ltd.**
1711, Centre 1, World Trade Centre,
Cuffe Parade, Mumbai 400 005, India.

Fill in the Mailing List form on our website
and receive, via email, information on
books, authors, events and more.
Visit: www.yogiimpressions.com

Telephone: (022) 61541500, 61541541
Fax: (022) 61541542
E-mail: yogi@yogiimpressions.com

 Join us on Facebook:
www.facebook.com/yogiimpressions

TITLES OF GAUTAM SACHDEVA
PUBLISHED BY YOGI IMPRESSIONS

Explosion of Love (2011)

The Buddha's Sword (2009)

Pointers from Ramesh Balsekar (2008)

pointers from
ramesh balsekar

dealing with life situations with
equanimity and peace of mind

gautam sachdeva

Also in Hindi and Marathi

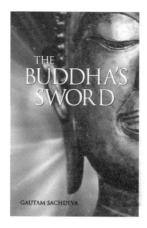

THE
BUDDHA'S
SWORD

GAUTAM SACHDEVA

Explosion
of
Love

Gautam Sachdeva

## The Sacred India Tarot

Inspired by Indian Mythology and Epics

**78 cards + 4 bonus cards + 350 page handbook**

*The Sacred India Tarot* is truly an offering from India to the
world. It is the first and only Tarot deck that works solely
within the parameters of sacred Indian mythology – almost
the world's only living mythology today.

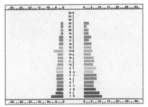
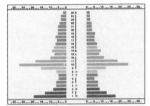